INDOOR PAUPERS

LIFE INSIDE A LONDON WORKHOUSE

BY

'ONE OF THEM'

PREFACE BY PETER HIGGINBOTHAM

CONTENTS

PREFACE

Indoor Paupers, published at the end of 1885, is a unique volume. It is the only book-length, first-hand account of workhouse life as seen through the eyes of an inmate. That this should be the case may in itself seem rather surprising. Twenty years earlier, the sensation caused by journalist James Greenwood's *A Night in a Workhouse* – a series of salacious articles published in the *Pall Mall Gazette* recounting his stay in the tramp ward of the Lambeth workhouse – had demonstrated the Victorian public's appetite for exposés of 'low life'. Although a number of other 'social explorers' – mostly middle-class journalists, novelists, social reformers, and the just plain curious – had subsequently followed in Greenwood's footsteps and published descriptions of their experiences, the personal reminiscences of those who became workhouse inmates out of sheer necessity are few and far between. Why should this be? Perhaps relatively few workhouse inmates would have been able to write at such length, especially in what one reviewer of the book called the author's 'easy and expressive style'. Even those with the necessary education or talent would probably have had more pressing concerns, or could not have imagined that anyone would be in the slightest bit interested in reading about experiences that were then relatively commonplace and viewed by many as unsavoury.

Other than his gender, the anonymous author of *Indoor Paupers* reveals little about himself. Likewise, the institution which he entered is not identified other than it being located in London. 'One of Them' is clearly a man of some education – perhaps not the usual run of workhouse inmates. So much so, in fact, that following the book's publication, at least one reviewer (from *The Law Times*) felt obliged to obtain 'some corroborative evidence that the publishers have not themselves been deceived by some fraudulent person.'

My own curiosity about the author of *Indoor Paupers* and of the establishment he described led me to contact the book's original publishers, Chatto & Windus, now part of the Random House group. The author's original contract still exists but, despite his being long-dead, the company still holds to its agreement of anonymity and declines to reveal the identity of 'One of Them'. However, on further delving into the company's archives, now held at Reading University, I discovered him to be one John Rutherford who, at the time of submitting his manuscript to Chatto in early November 1885, was a resident of the Poplar Union workhouse in East London. Rutherford, then aged sixty-one, had entered the workhouse during the previous July and presumably composed his text over the course of the following months. Chatto offered him sum of £20 for the copyright of the work, which Rutherford accepted, and within a week his manuscript had been despatched to the printers. He departed from the workhouse on 18 November and in January 1886 his author's complimentary copies of the published book were despatched to him at 16 Strafford Street, Westferry Road, Millwall. Little else is known about John Rutherford – assuming that to be his real name. He apparently never made a personal visit to the publisher's offices, with the payment being arranged through an intermediary.

As well as its narrative of the daily round in the workhouse, brought to life by descriptions of the other inmates and their backgrounds, Rutherford makes a number of serious allegations about the misconduct amongst workhouse officers – one of the reasons, perhaps, for his demand for anonymity. What is perhaps most striking about *Indoor Paupers*, though, is that the picture it paints is often very much at odds with the conventional image of workhouse inmates being wholly oppressed and submissive. Instead, they employ whatever means – or guile – they can in order to make institutional life more tolerable.

A view of the Poplar Union workhouse.

Although Rutherford's book made relatively little impact at the time – it was not reprinted and original copies are now quite rare – his work provides a unique insight into life inside a London workhouse in the 1880s.

Peter Higginbotham, January 2013.

CHAPTER I.
INTRODUCTORY.

I SHALL say nothing here of how I was driven to destitution. That is a tale in itself, and in all probability will be told ere long in a court of law.

My last month of freedom was a terrible one. At its commencement I found myself homeless, with a fairly good suit on my back, and a few shillings in my pocket. The cash was soon spent—chiefly in clean beds, which are expensive things in London. Then such articles of clothing as I could dispense with were sold or pawned. In this way I got through about ten days. The following three weeks were spent—alternately a night, or perhaps two in succession, in the streets, and the next two in a casual ward, want of sleep and absolute hunger compelling me to take shelter in the latter.

Outside of the casual ward, I passed the days in the Parks at the West End of London. Fortunately for me, it was summer, warm, and for the most part dry, or I should not now be recounting what befell. I was very far from being the only homeless and destitute individual living, or, rather, trying to hang on to life, in this way, at the same date. I am convinced from what I saw, especially far on in the night, that there were over a thousand persons doing much the same as myself—with a single exception. Most of these people knew how to *mouch* or beg with skill and effect, while I could not beg at all, and indeed never could bring myself to make the attempt.

During the day the open spaces of the Parks—particularly of St. James's—were absolutely black with these gentry, laid at full length on the grass, with their backs to the sun. On one occasion I could count no less than one hundred and nine thus stretched out, and in sight at the same time, within two hundred yards of Piccadilly. Here they slept soundly for long hours, and were thus enabled to rouse fresh and strong for the nightly prowl. It was a thing I could never do. I often felt sleepy enough during the night, between twelve o'clock and three; but, as day drew on, the drowsiness invariably vanished.

So long as the light lasted, I could not rest for any length on the Park benches. Bitter thoughts acting on an irritable temperament kept me constantly on the move, and thus wore me out while the sun was yet high. Thus I was compelled to betake me to a resting—place during the only time I could rest—that is, the night—long hours before it would have been necessary, had I husbanded my strength; and in consequence I felt the heavy night dews far more than I otherwise would have felt them.

One thing seemed to me then, as it seems still, very remarkable. I did not feel the want of food as other people. There was none of that torturing gnawing in the stomach which I have heard others describe. I grew faint and dizzy from long fasting, and that was all. Perhaps this ought to be attributed to the fact that I was continually drinking copiously at one or other of the public fountains; indeed, I was careful to confine my wanderings within easy distance of a few of them. At night, however, I seldom drank at all.

My place of resort, by preference, during the hours of darkness was one of the niches of Blackfriars Bridge. I tried London Bridge, but did not like it nearly so well. The niches there are not so deep, while the fencing walls are lower. On these two bridges, on the seats along the Thames Embankment and on those in Trafalgar Square, the homeless of the metropolis are allowed to pass the night without being ordered to move on by the police. The places named are the only ones where they are permitted to rest at night; and a great privilege they consider it, as I can assure my readers.

The more reckless know how to find better shelter by climbing the Park railings, or getting into empty houses, or such as are in the course of building—running some risk, of course. The bridges, the embankment, and Charing Cross are resorted to by the more tame and law-abiding.

Vagrants sleeping on a bench on London's Embankment.

At the same time there are great numbers who do not rest at all, but spend the live-long night in traversing the streets. I have more than once taken a round, lasting from half-past ten to four in the morning, and I never paced a hundred yards without passing the wanderers of the night in couples or threes. These were not what may be termed *professional wanderers*, be it well understood, but in all cases persons in the same condition as myself.

The Thames Embankment is too much exposed to be much frequented, except by persons who, to use a vulgar but expressive phrase, are cut on the loose. Perhaps the seats opposite the National Gallery are the most comfortable of any; but I did not learn that night-wanderers were at liberty to rest their weary forms upon them until my month of suffering was nearly out.

Persons of both sexes and all ages crowd the niches of the bridges named, and the seats of Trafalgar Square. I have seen children of eight to twelve there; plenty of youths, and even grey-headed women. I have noticed one elderly woman in particular in the same niche, and nearly on the same spot, every time I paid a nightly visit to Blackfriars Bridge—that is about seven times in three weeks—and have reason to believe that she spent the whole of these twenty-one nights in the same spot.

As to the numbers sheltering in the places named, there are, if I remember aright, eight seats in Trafalgar Square—one row down below by the fountains, the other on the footway above each seat will accommodate eight persons with ease; but when closely packed, ten or even twelve. On the few occasions when I saw them after midnight they were crowded thus. Moreover, there were some scores of persons lying in all positions on the bare stones of the square, just behind the lower row of seats, and close to the sheltering wall. I should say that never fewer than one hundred and twenty persons rest themselves here during the summer nights.

A much larger number was always to be found on the bridges. Each of the five-seated niches of Blackfriars Bridge is capable of seating twenty to twenty-five persons, but I never saw more than two quite full. Some are preferred to others, according to the direction of the wind. If the breeze from the river blow directly into a row of niches, they become intolerable to all but the hardiest. I have counted two hundred and fifteen persons at one time crouching on Blackfriars Bridge, and one hundred and fifty on London Bridge.

On no occasion, however, did I see them at their best—or, if the reader prefers it, worst—as regards thronging; that is, to say, on Saturday nights. There are several reasons why the bridges should contain more wanderers on that night than on any other. It is pay-night with thousands upon thousands, and drinking-night above all others; therefore just the night when mouthing pays best. The craft, therefore, is plied unremittingly while the taverns remain open, and as long after as there are revellers about the streets. It is not until the last of these revellers have disappeared from such haunts as the Haymarket that the mouchers betake them to the bridges, in anticipation of certain good things on Sunday morning.

Men sleeping under the arches of a London bridge.

Early on that morning, as I have been assured by many, the leading members of a truly charitable association make the round of London and Blackfriars Bridges, distributing tickets to all the homeless whom they find there. These tickets being presented in the proper quarter—somewhere in the Borough—entitle the holders to a substantial breakfast, which includes a liberal allowance of meat.

But the reason just given is not the only one why wanderers prefer to pass Saturday night on the bridges. There are a good many places in London where free breakfasts and teas are given to the destitute on the sabbath solely—the only conditions attached to the gift being, that the recipients shall join in several hymns, and listen to a few prayers and an exhortation of indefinite length. I may observe that they do not dislike the hymns, but would much prefer breakfast and tea without prayer or exhortation.

But the bridges are no pleasant places of sojourn, even on the finest nights of midsummer. There is the keen air from the river piercing one through; and the heavy dews penetrate the half-starved and scantily clothed bodies to the bone. Meanwhile the stone seats abstract the heat from the body in a way acutely painful. From twelve o'clock forward the wretches begin to shiver and crowd together for warmth, dozing however, and even sleeping, as they sit upright. They must not venture, however tempted, to lie down, or even recline; for the policemen on the beat peer round with lighted lanterns at frequent intervals, to rouse up those who abandon the upright position, and, if it be necessary, to move them on.

Towards morning most are in pitiful plight—chilled all over, and longing intensely for the sun to rise and warm them. I write from bitter experience.

A night on the bridges is bad at best; but it becomes something awful in a drizzle. This is generally borne with patience by the wanderers, who are too weary and weak to care to move, unless under absolute compulsion. I myself have sat under a three hours' drizzle, nor did I notice above two quitting the shelter during the whole time. A temporary squall, even though accompanied by heavy rain, is not so bad. Here the shower falls slanting—very much so in most cases—and one can generally escape all but a few drops, by choosing one's corner judiciously, according to the direction of the blast.

But when the rain comes down direct and heavily, and for long hours at a time, as I have had it, there is nothing for it save to rise and be off through the streets, keeping on the leeward side, and stealing odd rests in doorway and entry while the policeman is out of the way.

I had two such nights. The rain began about half-past twelve, and lasted, without intermission, for exactly eight hours in the first instance. It was my first night in the streets. I knew nothing of the ways of wanderers at that date, and found myself in the vicinity of the East London Hospital, in Mile End Road, when the rain began. Having been afoot and without food from early morning of the preceding day, I was unspeakably weak and worn, hardly able to drag my legs after me. Fortunately the police were kindly, and allowed me to rest at intervals in one or other of the numerous covered passages thereaways. Still the long hours, until the pawnbrokers' shops opened, were very trying. On that occasion my coat went, an old thing that I picked up for a few pence in the neighbourhood having to do duty instead.

But, miserable as was the night, I was far from being the only outcast afoot in Mile End Road. There were not less than fifteen *unfortunates* in the same predicament: there were a husband and wife; there were a number of half-grown lads; and there were quite a dozen men of all ages. It seemed odd to me then that a group would cower under the same shelter for an hour at a time, without a single one exchanging a word with another. However, I soon grew used to that sort of thing. It is the rule among people on their introduction to the final stage of ruin—the streets. They shrink from companionship and conversation. I have repeatedly sat, one among twenty, on Blackfriars Bridge for weary hours without hearing a single word spoken.

I had a second and worse night a little later. The rain began earlier, came down more heavily, and kept at it longer. It scattered the houseless from the bridges, but not immediately nor willingly. I was even weaker and more fatigued than on the first occasion. But this time the policemen I encountered were ubiquitous, pouncing upon me wherever I paused with their eternal 'Move on!' and keeping me trotting under the shower until I was ready to drop with cold, fatigue, wet, and famine.

How I got through the ensuing day I cannot now remember. The following night, however, one of my legs gave way completely, becoming inflamed, perfectly crimson all round from heel to knee, and swollen besides to double the natural size. I could then fully understand that species of old-world judicial torture, termed 'the boot.' My own boots were making me suffer it at every stride. It was a fearful time!

Worse still, this night to be remembered was followed by a day of incessant squalls of the fiercest kind—carrying hail as well as rain with them—which rendered it equally impossible for me to try the Parks or sit on any of the bridges. I was kept afoot until I was well-nigh mad with manifold torture. I spent the ensuing night in a casual ward, driven into it in spite of my rooted repugnance to such places. The piece of dry bread I received there for supper was the first food I had tasted for thirty-six hours. And on two occasions afterwards I fasted quite as long, and was relieved in precisely the same way.

However, before I say my last of the bridges, it is but fair to remark that all my experiences of them were not evil. On two different occasions—once in the evening and once again in the early morning—I have been beckoned from my seat by different working-men, whom I never saw before, and have never seen since. Each of these men insisted on taking me to an adjacent coffee tavern, and giving me a meal, forcing a few pence into my hand besides.

The strangest assistance, however, that I received came from one of the strangest characters I ever encountered. He was a religious enthusiast or maniac, which you please. Constantly afoot, he only paused here and there to warn people to repentance, and to beg a little food. In the towns he spent his nights in the streets; in the country, in the fields. He carried with him a piece of tarpaulin and a sack. When he felt in need of rest, he selected a sheltered corner of a field, crept into his sack, rolled his tarpaulin round him and it, and so bivouacked in defiance of all weathers. He told me, and I fully believed, that he had slept thus among the snows of the mountains of Glamorganshire. He was stout and hale, though with hairs beginning to grizzle, and seemed capable of bearing any amount of fatigue. The man's skull was large, and the face a fine open one. His heart, too, in spite of his mania, was in the right place. This person picked me out from a number, and insisted on sharing an *al fresco* breakfast with me. It was composed of odds and ends. All, however, were good; and there was enough and to spare—the overplus being pressed upon my acceptance. This done, the man stood up, and thundered out his accustomed warning to the passengers, of whom there were many; for it was now between five and six in the morning, and crowds were hastening across the bridge to their places of employment. Afterwards he gathered his bundle upon his shoulder and went his way; and I saw him no more.

These three pieces of unasked-for aid come to me, each one in the very nick of time. As to my experience of the casual wards of London—six of which I entered, and in three of which I spent successive Sundays—I am afraid I can say but little in their favour. They are all harsh, though in various degrees, that of Marylebone being the harshest of any. Here the casuals are confined in separate cells. They have each four pounds of oakum to pick, with not a single one of the usual aids. 'We do not allow you to beat the oakum here,' remarked the taskmaster in truculent tones to myself. And every particle of the work has to be done before the casual is released.

There is a metal pot, with a cover, in every cell; but the cover does not fit tight, and the pot, which serves as latrine, emits in consequence a most noisome smell. If ever the cholera visits London, I am quite sure that it will make an early appearance in Marylebone Workhouse, and not spare the inmates.

'Coffin' beds in the casual ward of a London workhouse.

On Sunday I was here locked up in solitary confinement as on the Saturday. No book, not even a Bible, was supplied. I received my modicum of bread and water on that day, and was allowed to lie down at seven o'clock. I might have been a dog, for all the authorities of the place cared. I must confess that I whiled away quite five hours of the Sabbath by completing that portion of my task which I found it impossible to finish on the Saturday. But nobody took the slightest notice of the matter. So much for the casual ward of highly civilized Marylebone.

I spent a second Sunday in the workhouse—St. Saviour's, I think they call it—situated in Southwark Bridge Road. Here, for some inexplicable reason, all casuals receive breakfast in bed. It consists of bread and warm gruel, and I was exceedingly grateful for the latter. It was the first warm food I had tasted for days.

Sunday, however, left the casuals as little cared for here as in Marylebone. They were congregated together in a heap, and left to amuse themselves as best they might, the favourite occupation being to tease two or three who showed themselves peculiarly irritable. The graceless crew—for a graceless crew it was—however, had generous spirits in it. I was utterly unable to get through my four pounds of oakum on the Monday. Seeing this, and pitying me, half-a-dozen of my temporary companions took it between them and performed the task for me.

In this place I met two persons whom I shall not soon forget. One was a professional jockey, who had been in the service of several foreign magnates, the Duc d'Aumale among the rest. He was a master of his craft—that was evident—and moreover could speak French and German fluently. But his love of the bottle had ruined him irreparably. He was living among and upon coachmen and grooms. In the casual ward he contrived to improve his fare, by lending his practised hand to the paupers appointed to tend a few horses belonging to the place, as I have cause to remember, for he shared the meat he received in return with myself. (This person, I have reason to believe, committed suicide a few weeks later.) The other fellow was one who had figured conspicuously in a noted trial, with evil consequences for himself. He was a clever and daring rascal—a man whose abilities, natural and acquired, might have won him fortune had they been properly used. But here he was, with sight almost gone, and destined to total blindness at no distant date, groping his way about, and as helpless for any purpose as a child.

My third Sunday was spent in Paddington Workhouse. The day was very different from what I found it elsewhere. The guardians recognised the fact that even casuals, however degraded, are possessed of souls; therefore, such of them as belong to the Established Church are invited to attend divine service, if it so please them. In addition, abundant reading, and that of a kind to suit their taste, is provided for all.

14

Strange tales have been told of the recklessness and ruffianism of the wretches who haunt casual wards. So far as I could see, there is little foundation for them. My fellows in these retreats were, as a rule, utterly broken down and spiritless, retaining hardly anything of the man save the shape, with no craving but for food and shelter, and no ambition except to hang on to life a little longer. With what deference they hung on every word of the ward-master; and how respectful they were to his indoor-pauper assistants! Above all, how insolent were the same pauper assistants to the miserable casuals! How they bullied, reviled, swore at, and otherwise showed their intense contempt for the miserable casuals! The latter were evidently in their eyes not human beings like themselves, but something infinitely meaner. These pauper assistants, indeed, were far and away the most blackguardly and ruffianly persons that I met in the casual ward. Among the casuals themselves, there was none of that intense eagerness for ribald anecdote and narrative with which they have been credited ever since the publication, years ago, of a certain clever and highly coloured sketch of a night in such a place. Their life, and the hardships to which it is incident, have knocked the ribald spirit, and indeed spirit of any kind, completely out of them. It is only in the over-fed and under-worked that riotousness is rampant. It can hardly find a congenial seat under the seedy garments and in the empty stomach of the genuine casual.

In the vagrant ward I found the staple of conversation still the same, viz., how to raise a few coppers or obtain a little food during the day; and how to escape recognition, and consequent imprisonment for three days in the ward, by any of the visitors of the Local Government Board who may happen to call.

Here, I may remark, that the acquaintance of the general run of casual with the routine of duty and the whereabouts of these officers at any particular moment is simply astonishing. How they obtain it is a mystery. But that they do obtain this information is unquestionable. There are four such officers, and they have thirty-two workhouses under their supervision. Each of these establishments must be visited thrice a week—twice in the morning and once at night. I was told all this, on the Friday evening that I entered Marylebone Vagrant Asylum, by a fellow-casual, who further stated that one particular officer—giving his name—was to visit the ward in which I sat on that particular evening. And as lie told, so it happened.

As to the confinement for three days by an officer of any casual whom he meets more than once in a month—that is certainly carried too far. In my limited experience, I met a poor fellow who was undergoing this punishment for the third time in succession within a single fortnight. It is no light punishment either—more severe, I have been informed, than that of any metropolitan prison; for, while the food is more scanty, the labour is heavier. The gaol-bird has only three pounds of oakum to pick in the day, while the casual must do four pounds. It is as much as saying to the latter, 'Your efforts to remain at large and make your way into employment are the very worst offences you can perpetrate against society. Go into the workhouse, or commit some offence that will place you for a time in prison, and we will be much more lenient with you. But we do not want you prowling about our streets, and especially disfiguring our public pleasure-grounds by your wretched and hated appearance.' And this is precisely how the casual interprets the severity of the system to which he is subjected. Everybody, indeed, is equally pitiless to him, seeming to think that he has no business at all in the world, and that the sooner he takes himself out of it the better. And here I cannot help offering a suggestion, that frequently occurred to my mind in those days, to this eminently humanitarian England of ours, in this most humanitarian of all centuries, the nineteenth. It is this: why not collect all the casuals of the metropolis in a heap, on a given day, and shoot them down like wild beasts? Such an act would be real mercy to most of them. And then, you see, it would be such a saving to the rates, while—consideration as grave—it would prevent the

16

elegant idlers of the Parks from having various senses offended, as now, by the presence in the said Parks of the vagrant.

Vagrants asleep in London's Green Park.

Towards the close of the fourth week I found that I was subjecting myself to hardship and suffering to no purpose. Every hour that passed rendered the prospect of retrieving my affairs more hopeless. My garments were getting repulsive in appearance, and myself weak and wan to the last degree. But what was I to do? There were three alternatives before me—to walk the streets till I dropped, to become a casual permanently, or to take refuge in the workhouse at once.

The first of the alternatives mentioned was sheer insanity, and the second still worse. Three months of the life of a vagabond, as I saw by many examples, were enough to spoil a man utterly for anything else. They deprived him of all the nobler instincts and ambitions, and reduced him to the condition of the beasts of prey; the meaner beasts, be it observed, the furtive depredators— the rat and that sort of creature, with at least a little of the fox.

As to the workhouse, it was literally burying one's self alive. There was a fourth alternative, which I need not name, and which too many wanderers in the like desperate straits have embraced. But that never for a single moment crossed my mind. My strongest defence against the idea was, I admit, not of the highest quality. I had enemies whom I believed to be unscrupulous; and in order to circumvent them, I determined to live, remembering the old adage, 'While there is life there is hope.' But, as for me, there was no means of living and retaining my native powers outside the walls of the workhouse. So I mastered my repugnance to the place at length, and entered; and not one moment too soon.

It took me a whole night to make up my mind. When this was accomplished I was five or six miles distant from the workhouse which was bound to receive me. I spent quite three hours in covering the distance. My legs could hardly carry me along. I was obliged to pause frequently, and take a seat wherever one was to be had. But the rising again was something to think of—a slow and painful operation, seldom to be completed without the aid of a passer-by to help me to my feet. Then the first few steps were made in misery; feet, legs, my whole body, in fact, aching.

I found the process of becoming an indoor pauper easy enough. The relieving officer was kindly disposed, did not ask any superfluous question, and gave the order without demur. This took place just inside the gate. I was then ushered into the receiving ward, a detached building of two floors, in charge of a pauper. Here males, who present their order after the departure of the doctor, spend the rest of the day and the following night, nobody being passed over to the body of the house until examined by the medical man and pronounced free from skin-disease.

I was then taken to the bath-room and treated with, what was to me a luxury indeed, a dip in clean warm water. Then my own clothes were taken away, folded up and ticketed, while I was supplied with a workhouse suit. In the process the ward-man made a merit of supplying me with an extraordinarily good suit, and a still greater merit of letting me have a flannel singlet. This latter act he took care to tell me was a very great favour indeed, and therefore, well worth a bit of tobacco or a copper. And he got a penny—my last—a part of a small sum raised the evening before by the sale of a handkerchief. But the old fellow lied in every particular. The singlet, as it turned out, was a portion of the ordinary workhouse dress, while the clothes were so bad that the taskmaster ordered them to be changed for better ones a few days later. Thus my first experience of the place was, to be victimized.

Immediately after my change of clothing the doctor made his appearance. I passed the scrutiny successfully, and was immediately transferred to the house, being sent incontinently to the stone-yard, a place where, according to rule, all males must spend their first week. There was no stone-breaking, however. Myself and about ten others were employed for the rest of the week in removing the hemp from a lot of telegraph-wires. There was no hurry over the job—very much the contrary—but plenty of chatter and larking when the taskmaster was out of sight. There was not a little skulking, too, at all times. The last—the skulking—I soon found was common all over the place, most of the inmates vying with one another as to which of them should do the least possible amount of work, and with much success, I must confess. It would require a dozen officers, each with the eyes of an Argus, to watch these gentry and keep them up to even a decent seeming of industry.

The following Monday I was transferred to the oakum-shed, where I have remained ever since, and where the task imposed is anything but killing. The younger men are supposed to pick four pounds of oakum, and the older two pounds. A few of the latter do their work regularly—only a few, however; but no young man that ever I saw completed his four pounds.

Of course the quantity of oakum a man can pick depends on the quality of the stuff, and at times the latter is of such sort that it can almost be blown asunder. But, good or bad, it is always the same. The oldsters, as a rule, pick a pound or a pound and a half, and the youngsters one pound to three, according to the elasticity of their several consciences.

Workhouse inmates picking oakum.

My great apprehensions respecting the house were, first, how I should be received by the other inmates; and, second, lest any of them should recognize me. With regard to the latter, I have been agreeably disappointed. So far, I have not met a single person who was acquainted with me even by sight. As to the rest, I found plenty of bullying and trickery going on; but it was soon seen that I was no fit subject for either practice, and, with a few exceptions, the bullies and tricksters have kept aloof.

A fortnight passed before I could realise my position or recover the balance of my mind. The latter had been sadly disturbed by the fearful experiences already sketched. However, when I settled down, though acknowledging to myself that there were worse places than the workhouse, one idea took possession of my mind, and held its place to the end. It was to get out of the workhouse, and resume my position in society as soon as possible.

After deep and anxious cogitation reaching over weeks, could see but a single way to attain my wish. It was to pen a small volume respecting indoor paupers and the life they led. The subject, it was clear to me, was deeply interesting, and could not but interest the public, if properly handled. Better still for my purpose, it had never been dealt with before; at least, from the points of view from which I saw it. And these points, let me remark, seem to me the only ones from which it can be properly surveyed. Further, a volume on indoor paupers, written by one of themselves—and every line in a workhouse—could hardly fail to excite curiosity. In short, such a book, if at all well written, was bound to prove successful. And such a book I determined to write.

Every day that passed supplied me with new materials—giving me broader and more accurate information respecting the place in general, and bringing me in contact with additional individuals of strange history.

I was soon provided with pens, ink, and paper, chiefly by the aid of a humble and attached friend. But the time in which to write—there lay the difficulty. The indoor pauper spends many hours—ten in summer and eleven in winter—locked up in his dormitory. Nine hours in summer and eight in winter are spent in the workshops. About an hour and a half more are spent at meals. Quite an hour is frittered away at various times. So that there remains hardly more than an hour and a half daily for writing—this on week-days. Sunday offered greater leisure. Duly allowing for meals and the time spent in the single church service, there were about ten hours at my disposal in summer, to be shortened to nine after September 25. Thus I should have nineteen hours weekly to myself.

However, I soon found nineteen hours weekly, subject as they were to constant interruption, far too little, so I fell into the habit of eking out this space by writing in bed. The trick was easy enough during the long days of midsummer; but towards the end of August the light began to grow annoyingly short. Yet even this difficulty did not seriously interfere with my plans, the principal of which consisted in getting through my work within a certain time. Securing a bed under a window looking due south, a little practice showed me that I could write legibly when there was light enough to enable me to place words and lines in their proper position. A very small amount of light sufficed. I could execute my work well in a clear starry night. But when the moon was up I was happy, since I could scribble just as readily as in the daylight. In fact, a very large portion of this volume has been produced 'in the dark,' physically speaking, though I presume to think no otherwise.

CHAPTER II.
SELF-CONSIDERED VICTIMS.

TAKING the indoor paupers of this house, whom I may regard as typical of the indoor paupers of all great towns, I question if five in a hundred will ever be found to owe their degradation to anything save their own misdeeds. I make the assertion calmly and deliberately, and after protracted investigation. This is a fact which the majority of indoor paupers make no attempt to conceal. As to the minority, men have come to me of themselves, or have been brought by others, as the victims of downright villainy. In all cases their stories were plausible in the extreme, and many very touching; but there were very few indeed which did not break down under investigation. There was always a little something carefully suppressed, which came out, much against the will of the grievance-mongers, under close sifting—a piece of vice, folly, or downright criminality, which sufficiently accounted for every step of the ruin that followed its perpetration.

The truth is, the general run of indoor paupers richly deserve their fate, and a great many seem to like it better than any other. There are dozens of men under my view at this very moment who have been removed from the house and been given opportunities of making themselves comfortably independent out of doers—many of them several times over. Yet here they are again as hopeless and helpless as ever.

The number who blame the guardians as the main cause of their lot is astonishing. These people ignore the fact that the guardians did not bring them here in the first instance. All they think fit to remember is that, at one time or another after becoming indoor paupers, it occurred to them that, if they could but make a decent appearance outside, they would have a chance of employment. Accordingly they applied to the board for a suitable outfit, and received the answer generally given under the circumstances, viz., 'We will do what we can in a fair way to help you. Prove to us that you can secure employment, and you shall have all the outfit you require.'

As the grumblers, however, could not satisfy the condition imposed—and very properly—by the guardians, the outfit was denied. And for this reason, and no other, they credit the guardians with their ruin, and cherish undying animosity against them as the sole causes of it. It is curious that, while thus estimating and resenting the refusal, these gentry pronounce invariably that fellow-applicants who met with the like meed were rightly served. Thus they condemn themselves very completely, though they cannot see it.

Perhaps the denial of an outfit may seem hard now and again; but when one comes to see how often such grants have been misapplied, and how exceedingly seldom utilized, one will hardly venture to blame the guardians much. Still the fact is as I state. There is no workhouse in England wherein a proportion, often amounting to 10 per cent., of the inmates do not attribute their pauperism to the guardians.

A still greater number credit runaway wives with their introduction to the house; and these also condemn themselves without perceiving it. So long as the much-maligned partners clung to them, their homes were kept together, and husbands and children preserved from pauperism. But when the woman disappeared, it took but a short time—merely a few weeks—to break up the home and send the man and his children into the house.

Looking at this fact, one cannot help asking one's self, Are the absconding women so very much to blame? Shiftless and weak as such husbands are—often utterly worthless into the bargain—what woman of strong feelings would continue to love and cherish and waste her prime on one of them? Is there any of them worth such a sacrifice? The fact that the runaway wife kept things together so long, and that matters went to the dogs completely when she vanished, proves that she must have possessed a number of fine qualities. It is not hard to see

24

wherefore she took the one fatal step. Nor has that step led to a life of sin in the majority of instances, or been taken until it was the only means of escaping the degradation and virtual imprisonment of the workhouse. On fairly examining the conduct of the runaways, it will be found that, for the most part, they clung to their families to the last moment. Then, seeing close at hand the bitter end of the husband's inveterate weakness and worthlessness, and shrinking from the life of indoor paupers, they returned to their relatives or went to service.

Even where the worst occurred, there is much to extenuate. A few feet from me sleeps a man once well-to-do as a shopkeeper. He is barely forty, but already a pauper who is not likely to be anything else. He ruined himself by incorrigible vices. He was a betting man and a profligate in every sense. Moreover, nobody living could place the slightest trust in anything he ever said, or rely upon him in any way. His wife put up with him for years upon years. At last, the workhouse, with its miserable prison life, being full in view, this woman, several years her husband's junior—fine-looking too, full of vigorous life and womanly feelings, and exasperated by a long course of something worse than neglect—gave way to the solicitations of an old sweetheart who had remained single for her sake; and, taking the youngest and most helpless of her children, emigrated with this old lover. The husband incontinently broke up house and became an indoor pauper. The fact that he had held a respectable position, and that his nearest relatives still filled respectable positions, disposed the guardians to befriend this man. Once and again he obtained a permission, occasionally granted in hopeful cases, to go out into the world and make a home, leaving his children behind him. On each occasion he went direct to a situation, receiving a suitable outfit from the guardians. On each occasion he made not the slightest attempt to make a home; and on each occasion the guardians were compelled to have him arrested and sent to prison for a term.

Here he is now, a hopeless pauper, blaming wife and guardians as the cause of his ruin, though it is perfectly clear to anybody of common sense that he compelled both to do what they did. It is a typical instance, a little stronger, perhaps, than many, but not half so strong as some.

Another specimen of the wife-deserted indoor pauper is a fine powerful fellow, in the prime of life, with plenty of ability and education to back it. He is an artisan, and a skilful one, in most branches of iron-work. Boiler-making, iron-shipbuilding, fitting, etc., are occupations in which he has no superior. He can turn his hand to anything almost in an iron factory, be it rough or smooth. Consequently, he is precisely the man who should never be out of employment for even an hour.

His temper is a happy one, full of fun and joke, and he has many fine and taking qualities. A lie he never utters; his courage is sure, and he may be relied on to back his friends in trouble to the last. Generous and sympathetic, too, as well as handsome, frank, and fearless, he is just the man one would think to fasten upon himself the life-long affections of a wife; yet he has done precisely the reverse.

For a couple of years past he has been one of that exceedingly troublesome and worthless class, the 'Ins and Outs,' of which more in another place, and all in consequence of the predominence in him of certain impulses. He cannot resist the attractions offered by a jovial group in the tap-room; still less can he resist the blandishments of a new and buxom female acquaintance. And in order to enjoy the society of the one and the other, he allows himself to be tempted at times into forgetting that there is any distinction between *meum* and *tuum*: more is the pity.

He is adroit and wide-awake, and withal makes free with his neighbours' property in a conscientious sort of way. He will not possess himself of what is indispensable to a man, nor of anything the loss of which would produce serious, not to say irreparable, injury; and he would not perform even his little bits

26

of filching, if it were possible without them to enjoy his pet amusements. But the boon-companions, the merriment of the tap-room, the racy anecdote, and the rousing song—above all, the last brand-new pretty face—these are things without which life would cease to be worth the living, so far as he is concerned.

It needs hardly be said that he has not been 'copped'—as these people term arrest, conviction, and punishment—above twice in a long career, and that then he managed to escape the worst stigma and punishment under the guise of illegal possession or pawning. In fact, the gaol knows him rather as a misdemeanant than a criminal. He has never fallen into the hands of the police, except under circumstances such as to give his misdeeds a seeming of thoughtlessness and semi-accident, if I may be allowed to use such a term, and to take away the greater part of their criminality in the eyes of most people—his own eyes, of course, included.

Lookers-on seldom did more than laugh at his feats of appropriation, and pity him when they brought him to grief. Not so, however, his employers. Their ideas of such doings were of a sterner order. The result was that, long before his first 'copping' adventure came off, not one of them would give him a permanent job; though, as they well knew, a better hand was not to be found anywhere. He was only 'taken on' in emergencies, and probably no more frequently than he desired, as he never applied for a job, except when his credit had been pushed to the last extreme, when cronies as well as landlords had grown tired of his appeals for help, and when the resources of his numerous mistresses had been exhausted by his exactions.

Meanwhile, the house was kept together somehow by the exertions of the wife. She worked early and late—washing, sewing, mending—often far on into the night, never sparing herself in the least, and still idolizing the ne'er-do-well husband who, as she delighted to hope, would 'pull himself together one of these days,' and turn out quite a model husband and father. However, his ceaseless infidelities shook even her faith in him at last, and she lost heart. Then a hurt received from an irate husband laid the man up, and there was nothing for the family except to place the furniture for care with trusty friends and go into the house.

As an indoor pauper, Sam Hopkins won everybody—paupers, master, and guardians. His lot was made an easy one, to begin with. Then, when his health was restored, a former employer took pity on him, and Sam was put in the way of becoming a useful member of society.

Perhaps he might have done so, had Polly Hopkins remained as she had been. But the spell in the workhouse caught her in a critical state of mind and heart, and exposed her to a species of evil influence, to be described hereafter, precisely when she was in the mood to feel it most. She issued from the house with her principles as well as her affections sapped, with a feeling of degradation and shame, and of indignation also at the author of her temporary pauperism.

Polly learned to nag indoors, and being a very handsome woman, as suited the wife of such a man, to listen to compliment and solicitation from the young men about. Sam therefore relapsed all the more readily into his former habits. At this period took place one of his few 'coppings'—the imprisonment lasting but a few weeks. It was long enough, however, to send the family into the house for the second time, after disposing of the furniture as before.

In the old place, Sam played the old part, with the old effect on everybody—irate guardians included. Not so Polly. A few weeks more of indoor pauperism completely perverted her, and she made up her mind to waste no more of her days on such a husband. Inventing a plausible excuse, she went straight to the master, and begged a few hours' leave of absence. He, never dreaming of what was in her mind—how could he, all things considered, and with such a handsome husband and such fine children?—gave the requisite permission, and Polly hastened away without asking leave of husband or bidding 'good-bye' to the little ones. Poor Polly!

Out of doors, she went directly to a furniture-broker with a second plausible tale, and in his company visited, one after another, the various houses in which the furniture of her old home was stored. Here the parties, never doubting that she was acting under the orders of Sam, gave up the furniture at her request, and she sold every article to the broker for ready money. The cash in her pocket, she disappeared, and the detested workhouse saw her no more.

The act just mentioned put the finishing touch to the husband's demoralization and ruin. Wife and furniture lost, his difficulties became far too much for him, or, rather, he ceased to wrestle with them. Two of his children, being over fourteen, were soon disposed of—the boy to sea and the girl to service. Another boy, a child of eight or nine, remains; and whenever Sam feels in want of a few days in his accustomed haunts he discharges himself and boy. Perhaps he may obtain a few days' work; perhaps he is housed and fed by one or other of his old mates: in any case, the house is sure to see him back again ere half a week goes by. Thus he has been going on for a couple of years—ten days in the house and three to four out—with remarkable regularity. And so he bids fair to go on as long as he lives.

As to the wife, she passed through the hands of a series of paramours in rapid succession, until she descended into the streets. Nor was she interfered with in the least by the parochial authorities; for though a runaway husband who leaves wife and children on their hands is hunted down with untiring pertinacity, a runaway wife may do as she pleases, so long as her husband remains alive. So much for indoor pauper-husbands whose wives have deserted them.

A very different set of men, however, are the few husbands who are here through the death of cherished consorts. Such losses, as I have seen, break up men between forty-five and fifty-five very rapidly. They lose, or rather have lost long before, the qualities which keep households together. They are still quite capable of their daily labour; but the lonely hearth tries them too severely. They fly from it, indeed, into the workhouse, where they allow their thoughts to eat away their hearts in silence, moping about like senseless stocks, perfectly apathetic as respects their surroundings, utterly careless of the present, and living only in the past and the future—on the memory of lost happiness— on the hope of meeting those who have gone before into a better world. Those desolate old men are greatly to be pitied; but there are others even more desolate. Here is one. A few days will complete his seventieth year. He is short, but exceedingly broad, and must have been a powerful man in his time. With a fine, good-tempered-looking face and the most perfect simplicity of thought and manners—perhaps a little touched with servility— he wins one at once. Born of a peasant family in Worcestershire, he was bred a farrier, but left home and sweetheart for labour in London at an early age—as soon as he was out of his time, indeed—nor did he ever see her or any relative again. London drove them out of his thoughts. They ceased to write, and he never married; so when infirmities drove him into the house, he was entirely alone. Only the other day, a yearning of heart compelled him to write to one whom he had known forty-nine years earlier, but had never seen since, and never even heard of for almost the same period. The letter was returned, and the old man wept as he received it. It was the first time that he had realized his exceeding loneliness. He leaves no children behind him; he has no loved ones to meet him elsewhere. He is the most pitiable object of some three hundred male inmates.

Husbands pauperized through loss of wives! Yes; there are only too many here. But here also with them is a husband in the same condition through having too much wife. He is a fine, hale personage, a remarkably attractive and stately figure, sixty-nine to a day, yet hardly looking fifty, and evidently with twenty good years of life in him still. Nor does he lack the means of living comfortably outside either. His children, all of whom are settled in life, would do for him all that is requisite, were it necessary. Nay, he has enough of his own; but, after losing his first wife, who had been his companion in happiness for forty-five years, lie gave a termagant her place; and she drove him for shelter from her intolerable temper into the house in nineteen months.

CHAPTER III.
SUNDAY IN THE HOUSE.

SUNDAY is not a pleasant day in this house of ours. But as it is, in all its weary dreariness, so it was intended to be, and nothing else. The principle of its managers, that is to say, its guardians, has been from the first to make the place anything rather than an agreeable sojourn; and they have succeeded perfectly in realizing their intent.

It must be admitted that they are remarkably impartial here; though whether the impartiality be just, judicious, or even politic, are matters admitting of question. They treat every- body exactly alike: the old have no further privileges than those accorded to the young; and the best conducted and most useful stand on precisely the same footing, so far as the board of guardians is concerned, as the most worthless and blackguardly.

The Sabbath among us is a day of rest; emphatically so, or of stagnation rather. We have an hour longer in bed of a morning in the summer. We go to divine service once a day—that is, those of us who belong to the Established Church—and, immediately after supper, we have a troop of preachers let in upon us, who howl at us in the most uncompromising manner, without ever asking leave—very much against the will of many of us, indeed—from half-past six until bedtime. But more of these gentry hereafter.

Beyond this, it may be as well to state, no special provision is made for the spiritual wants of any of the numerous body of Dissenters. We have Baptists, Independents, Congregationalists, etc., among us, and a few Roman Catholics, too. The latter are duly looked to by their priest; but the Dissenters are on Sundays as though they were not. Even Mr. Spurgeon seems to have forgotten that the workhouse contains fellow-sectarians.

As to how we are to spend the eight hours, or thereabouts, that remain after meals, church, and howlers are disposed of, nobody, except ourselves and a few private friends outside; cares in the least.

The letter-writing of the place is not much: perhaps fifty letters a week may be received and replied to by its hundreds of inmates. Some of the replies are penned as soon after the receipt of the letter as circumstances will permit, but the greater number are deferred till Sundays. Then—always after church—about a dozen men wait their turn for the use of the solitary ink-pot and pen belonging to the apartment. This for the young men's hall. But it is much the same among the old men, and in each of the divisions into which the females are divided.

Letter-writing, however, occupies but a few inmates out of many; and these few for no more than half an hour or so apiece. They get through the rest of the time as the others get through the whole of it—anyhow, and mostly very drearily. The lazy fling themselves on the benches or on the floor in the corners, and doze through the day in a way utterly beyond the comprehension of people with active brains. But this plan of killing time is not peculiar to the workhouse. It is that invariably adopted by the sluggish of the lower classes when lack of funds, or the fact that the public-houses are closed, forbids them to resort to the only livelier means of getting through their leisure that they care to adopt.

Others lounge about the yard in listless fashion; and a most uninteresting promenade that said yard is. It is a broad quadrangle, girt in by the main building and its offices on three sides. The fourth side is bounded by a lofty wall, beyond which rises a high-level railway. We can hear the snorting of the engine, and we can see the steam and smoke, as a train passes; and that is the sum and substance of our intercourse with the world, apart from letters and from the visits of friends once a month.

This yard is covered with gravel from side to side. Not a leaf of grass or green thing is to be seen anywhere. The very sparrows seem to avoid the place. There is none of their chatter in the eaves, and none of their Sunday gambols on the ground. There is nothing whatever, indeed, to relieve the dull monotony of this dullest of haunts.

Here in the summer men lounge on the low wall of the dust-hole, or lie at full length, as in the halls, in the corners or close up against the walls on the sunny side; and here they stroll to and fro, at all seasons, in groups of twos, threes, and fours, but more frequently solitary. If they speak, it is with bated breath, in undertones, as if conscious that the very walls have ears to hear and tongues to tell to the authorities every word that falls. Nor is all this circumspection without reason; for the conversation is mostly in high criticism and censure of the shortcomings of the place, the poorness and scantiness of the food, the harshness—not to say tyranny—of the officials, and the general disregard displayed by the guardians of the wants and wishes of the pauper inmates. These, indeed, are the favourite themes of the talkers, indoors and out.

The solitary mope about, with downcast melancholy countenances, consuming their souls in the scathing fire of sad reflections and wretched memories.

Indoors there is more variety. There are loungers, single and in couples. There are readers also; only they themselves must provide the reading, unless they prefer something ultra-religious, which has lain in a waste-paper box for many months, the said waste-paper box and its contents being produced regularly every Sabbath. This, however, in the old men's hall only; and even these religious publications are the contribution of pious and charitable outsiders. All the guardians have done in this way is to place a single Bible in one of the windowsills, where it lies untouched from week's end to week's end, unless when a hypocrite of a certain class, of which we have several specimens, takes it up and appears to study it in order to make an impression on somebody, and so secure a selfish end. It may be an officer or a guardian that is thus aimed at, or it may be a few fellow-paupers whom the rascal wants to wheedle into trusting him, in order that he may obtain an opportunity for playing off a piece of characteristic chicanery.

We have one sedulous Bible reader in the young men's hall, a low-sized, swarthy fellow, with harsh features and an Italian name, evidently of the breed which one meets with halfway up the Apennines in the interior of Tuscany. And this man is notoriously the falsest inmate of the house: there is no believing a statement he makes, and no having dealings with him without being cheated. This is so thoroughly understood, that he and his Bible are left pretty much to themselves; and the Bible, in several instances, just because it is so regularly the companion of the other.

There are a few tattered novels about the room—only a few—which have been passing from hand to hand for months, continually losing leaves in the process, and which will continue so to pass until the last leaf has been consumed as a pipe light. Those in the very best state have lost covers, and the opening and concluding chapters as well. Others have three-fourths or a half of the pages remaining; while others, again, are reduced to a fourth or an eighth of their original size. But in all cases they are stuck to tenaciously by those who contrive to get hold of them, and read with as much attention as if there were life depending on it.

There are, perhaps, a dozen detached numbers of the cheapest illustrated publications—things relating the deeds of Claude Duval, Dick Turpin, and other desperadoes these among the younger inmates.

Newspapers, however, form the favourite intellectual fare. Three or four fortunate inmates receive a weekly journal regularly, and these are the men of standing of the place. They are deferred to, sought after, courted, and even paid in bits of bread or tobacco, for half-hour loans of the journals at their disposal.

Judging by the character of the newspapers among them, the politics of the indoor paupers are intensely radical. *Reynolds's* is preferred; then comes *The Dispatch*, and then *Lloyd's*. These three are common. Others appear occasionally; though, while we have odd specimens of county papers now and again, one of the great London dailies is hardly ever seen.

The indoor pauper, however, is simply content to read his journal. As a rule, he never talks about its contents, unless among them lies a divorce or breach-of-promise case, or a murder of more than usual interest.

So much for the readers.

Other men gather round the story-tellers, who are almost exclusively of the In-and-Out order, whose discourse is always of their own adventures, and who never by any chance have good to relate. On Sundays they dilate to attentive and sympathetic listeners concerning life on the road, and in the streets, prisons, casual wards, harlots, fences, thieving exploits, pugilistic encounters in the ring, ruffianly debauches, with their supplementary rows, dodging and squaring bobbies, and athletic competitions—the last being far and away the most innocent of the themes, even though they deal *ad libitum* with such personages as Jem Mace and Yankee Sullivan, and enlarge on how swell backers are 'done' by pre-arrangement between the competitors.

In spite, however, of all the methods of getting through the day just mentioned, the Workhouse Sunday, as we have it, is emphatically dull and dreary.

Some of the inmates, indeed—the married men—are allowed to pass an hour, immediately after divine service, with their wives and children; but in by far the majority of cases there is no pleasure in the interview. Such meetings take place under official supervision and in the sight of dozens. Tender feelings, therefore, must be suppressed, if such have survived the miserable period preceding the break-up of the home and the still more miserable—because in so many cases hopeless— imprisonment in the house that followed.

However, when the feelings are not tender, no great care is taken to suppress them at these interviews Husbands and wives, who bear one another grudges, take advantage of them to 'speak their mind,' and spend them for the most part in mutual recrimination.

The only features about these Sunday meetings between members of the same family that excite sympathy are witnessed in the cases wherein husbands and fathers, who have lost cherished wives, meet 'children of tender years. The way in which the youngsters fix themselves on a father's knees, and nestle in his breast with arms round his neck and cheeks against his, the way in which they lie there to the end of the interview, the melancholy aspect of the man, the silence of the group—for hardly a word is dropped among them—and the reluctance with which father and children tear themselves asunder, when they are compelled at length to quit the scene—are things that go straight to the heart.

I do not think that guardians are acting wisely in leaving indoor paupers to pass their Sundays as I have described. A hardening and deteriorating process is always going on among them, and most rapidly when they are most unemployed, that is, on Sundays. The Sabbath, indeed, which should be the day to elevate minds from the low level of weekday thoughts, does just the opposite among indoor paupers: it sharpens their original vices, and begets others to which they were strangers in another state. The listless and lazy become still more so; the filthy grow filthier still; while those who heretofore possessed merely a lurking and uncertain inclination towards certain vices have it strengthened and confirmed here. As for the positively vicious, they are rendered proud of their iniquitous doings, and therefore all the more ready and willing to repeat and improve upon them when opportunity serves.

Yet even in the very worst of these men there is left a little good which may be got at and expanded. This cannot be done by the single Sunday service, nor yet by the howling preachers. They care little for the former, and are notably contemptuous for the latter. They make a point, indeed, of laughing at sermon and good advice, when either attacks them directly, before comrades. It is bravado, of course; but even the most obviously simulated bravado has its effect on the listener and on the speaker too.

An open-air service at a workhouse.

A book, however, unlike advice and sermon, does not attack a man and rouse his hostility; it gets at him quietly. Its sentences reach him alone, and are not conveyed to bystanders as well. There is, therefore, seldom or never aught stimulating him to hold the lessons it contains up to ridicule. And if its good be conveyed under cover of an interesting narrative, it cannot but prove beneficial.

A series of good stories, with high moral tone, perused Sunday after Sunday without break, cannot fail to make an impression on the most stolid, and compel them, first to admire the virtues as painted in action, and then to imitate them on their own account.

A good book—which does not mean a goody-goody book, by any means—is a good thing anywhere and under any circumstances; but to my thinking it never can be so good as in places like the workhouse and on Sunday. Here and then there is positively nothing whatever to prevent it from fixing its grasp firmly on the mind of the reader, but everything to aid. Men, indeed, are literally ravenous for literary food—that is, supposing them able to read at all—and will put up with almost anything in book shape that comes in their way.

I can safely assert that it would be a gain to the ratepayers in many respects, and a very decided aid to the officers, if every workhouse was provided with a small library of well-selected volumes—such as are published in great numbers for popular use by various societies at the cheapest rate. Twenty pounds would provide at least two hundred such volumes; and this number would suffice in most places. If not, there are plenty of people dwelling in every union who would gladly contribute in money or books to swell the collection. Nor would it be either difficult or expensive to keep such a library in working order. A small apartment to contain the volumes, a ledger to record the lendings and returnings, and a pauper librarian would suffice.

And the results? Besides the general one already specified, such a library would tend to render the paupers less discontented, less given to running in all directions with complaints against everything about them and against everybody above them, but chiefly far less liable to be influenced by firebrands, such as the one to be described elsewhere, who has proved himself an unmitigated nuisance to everybody concerned with the establishment.

And less discontented means a good many things besides—as more care of the property of the ratepayers, more industry in the workshops, and more decorum and geniality in conduct and conversation. In short, the library would pay for itself several times over in the course of a single year.

But to resume my account of our Sundays. Our church, like that of many another workhouse, remains unconsecrated—probably on account of the expense attending the ceremony. In consequence the sacraments cannot be administered therein. This is a great loss in many respects, and tends more than anything else to render the Church's services mere formalities to those attending them. Three or four on the verge of the grave, with their senses still strong, may think seriously of another and a better world, and do their best to prepare themselves seriously for it; but the masses never bother their heads with such considerations. During my stay on the young men's side, though brought in contact with hundreds, I have encountered a few hypocrites, but never a single really pious individual, though many of these so-called young men were over forty, and not a few past sixty.

The howlers, as I have already stated, close the Sunday with us; and they never do anything save howl. They rant and roar at the men before them collectively, but never attempt to get at individuals, except by distributing leaflets, which are seldom read and invariably consumed as pipe-lights. As to the rant itself, it is mostly miserable stuff, disjointed, rambling, headless and tailless, abounding in endless repetitions and in the most astounding rashness of assertion and ignorance also. The intellect of the howlers, indeed, seems to have fattened on the narrow-minded theology of past centuries, and never to have heard of modern scholarship or tolerance. Every sentence they utter smells of the brimstone-lake. No doubt they mean well; but thanks to their deficiencies of culture and judgment, their discourses, in result, are merely so many illustrations of the old saw respecting good intentions.

CHAPTER IV.
INS AND OUTS.

INDOOR paupers admit of many subdivisions. We have the old and the young, the hopeful and the hopeless, the married and the single, the permanent and the transitory, and, finally, a class by themselves—the Ins and Outs.

The class last named is a remarkably troublesome one. As a rule, its members are completely worthless to themselves and to everybody else. They leave the house at regular intervals, putting the officers to an infinity of trouble in the process; for precisely the same lengthy forms have to be gone through at every fresh exit and entry as at the first.

Some of these fellows go out to a job, keep at it as long as it lasts, lay in good stores of tobacco at the end, and then spend every farthing left of their earnings in a topping spree,' lasting one to three days, according to the amount received. Then hey for the workhouse, or 'spike,' once again! Here the blackguards recover from their debauch, and drown away the days until they are ripe for another job and another 'topping spree.'

Such fellows are exceedingly provoking. They are men varying in age from 21 or so to 45—all abounding in life and vigour, and, without exception, perfectly capable of maintaining themselves by their own labour. They prefer this sort of life, however, and are not to be roused out of it, as things legal go. They are quite shameless, laugh at the heaviest toils of the house as being, what they really are to them, the merest child's play. They stick to the place as if it were their rightful inheritance. So, indeed, they regard it, inside and out. When his spree is over, and one of these gentry is about to seclude himself once more for the usual period, he bids adieu to his outside cronies with the meaning explanation, 'I am going home, boys—home once more.'

The reasons adduced by these Ins and Outs for leading this sort of life are very convincing to themselves. The spike is infinitely cheaper and cleaner than the common lodging-house.

It saves their own clothing, and, when the thing becomes absolutely necessary, provides them with more. It 'doctors' them when their malpractices result in foul diseases. And though the food is poor, it is regular, and greatly superior, besides, to what they can hope for when out of work and depending on themselves.

Nor are the above advantages all. The Ins and Outs, without exception, are profligates in the extreme. Many of them are just the fellows to insinuate themselves into the good graces of thoughtless girls of the lower classes; and precisely the lads also to take base advantage of the trust. Most of them have illegitimate children, and not a few two or three, for whom the unfortunate mothers have to provide as best they can. It is obviously useless to sue the fathers. When such a fellow finds the agents of the law at his heels, he becomes an indoor pauper incontinently, and so justice is baffled.

There are twenty-five or thirty men of this kind in the house with me at the present moment, all exceedingly sociable and jolly in their own estimation; and in the estimation of everybody else. They are all full of fun and frolic, and as full of good stories of their own reckless doings.

Another and about as numerous a class of Ins and Outs, whose members come and go and come again even more frequently than the tiptop-spree fellows, are the mouchers or cadgers. These fellows are inveterate beggars, and have been so time out of mind; acquainted, therefore, with all the tricks and devices of the craft to which they belong, and remarkably skilful in practising them.

They are acquainted with the localities and regulations of every charitable institution in and about the metropolis, and with the address and personal peculiarities of every charitable individual within the same area. The latter—the personal peculiarities—form a matter as essential to them as the address, since by playing judiciously upon them—and nobody is so adroit in such practices as the workhouse cadger—they 'get at' the person and inside of his sympathies, with the effect that they are pretty certain to secure his very largest dole.

They are constantly laying plans and making excursions for the purpose of levying black-mail on institutions and individuals. If successful, they tell the whole story, with due exultation, on their return to the house. If they fail, they tell all the facts in precisely the same detail—giving manager of institution and benevolent person full credit and approval, too, for whatever keenness and dexterity they may have displayed in detecting and baffling this attempted knavery.

It is not often, however, that such fellows allow themselves to be detected and baffled. Nothing can surpass the ingenuity with which they set about their work, or the dogged perseverance with which they stick to it. A true moucher will never allow himself to be driven from his purpose by a first repulse, or a second, or even a third. He will try, and try again, varying his trickery on each occasion until he hits on the dodge which carries him through.

He will change his story and his appearance over and over—become a very Proteus, in fact. These artists, as I may be allowed to term them, can alter voice and distort features and limbs in the most extraordinary way, and they have always comrades handy to exchange garments with them for the time.

Now and again there are circumstances which keep the workhouse mouchers very busy in such expeditions as those alluded to. Not long ago a certain great personage, in the centre of a certain great city, became extraordinarily benevolent. Every moucher that made a morning call at a certain place, and told a suitable story there, was presented with five shillings. No searching questions were put; the tale was accepted as genuine, and the money given on the spot. The news spread as such news always spreads, and, in consequence, the place where the crowns were given away was besieged every morning by mouchers, chiefly from workhouses. Many of them applied for and received the dole several times over. But a change soon took place. The great person received an addition to his name, or rather two additions—a prefix and an affix; and immediately that this happened the five-shilling doles to mouchers were discontinued, and these worthies presented, instead, when they crowded the place as usual, with orders for admission to a neighbouring casual ward. They were disappointed, of course, but in no wise discontented or angered. They treated the refusal rather as a very good joke on the part of the great personage, and thought no more of it.

The more usual occupation of the workhouse moucher out of doors is to haunt the taverns on Saturday, Sunday, and Monday evenings. There they act as follows:—One of them will introduce himself to a group of carousers either as the ancient mate or as the comrade of an absent mate, or by his facetious capabilities, of which he is certain to have a good many, fully developed and thoroughly well practised. And once attached to a knot of men, the moucher sticks to it pertinaciously for the rest of the evening. Here he plays the parasite to the full extent of his abilities, giving coarsely amusing songs and recitations as often as called upon, and indulging in all sorts of monkey-tricks and ridiculous antics. His chief use, however, is to act as the butt of the company; and he submits to all sorts of practical jokes with unfailing patience and even good humour. Flour and red ochre sprinkled upon him, no matter how plentifully, never offend, provided they be followed by a few additional cups and coppers. Come what may in the shape of sharp practical joke, he 'grins and bears it' until his turn comes. This is when the party breaks up. Then our moucher attaches himself to the member thereof who is most unsteady on his legs, and carries him out of the way of his companions. In all probability he hands him over to a female harpy who has been waiting about. In any case he either clears the poor man's pockets himself, or assists in the operation; and when he is done with him he leaves him stretched at full length on the sideway; or even goes so far as to hand him over to the police for safety.

Mouching, as an alternative to indoor-pauper life, is not exclusively confined to individuals. Whole families practise it, taking their discharge with clock-like regularity once a week, spending the day in begging here and there in the most likely places, enjoying themselves the while on the proceeds, and returning at night to the shelter of the house. The proceeding, as followed by one particular person and his family, furnished a theme to one of the house-poets—for even the workhouse contains its versifiers—and the following stanzas were the result.

Hunky sings:

'Workhouse life is dreary—
    Gloomy as the grave:
Something much more cheery
    Once a week I'll have.
Workhouse fare is scanty;
    Workhouse fare is poor:
Something much more dainty
    Hunky must secure.
        Oh, the joys of cadging,
        Wife and kids at heels,
        No one can imagine
        Save the bloke that feels.

Once a week we cut it
    From the workhouse gate;
Then we gaily foot it
    In our robes of state.
Kids in garments tattered,
    Hunky with a tile,
Like himself, much battered,
    And his constant smile.

45

                    Oh, the joys, etc.

Round and round we trudge it,
        Careless of what haps;
Filling up our budget
        With all sorts of scraps.
Coppers, too, we gather
        In our worn-out hats;
Coppers all for father,
        Scraps for wife and brats.
                    Oh, the joys, etc.

Not when sunshine glows, sirs,
        Do I like my task;
Hail, or rain, or snow, sirs—
        That is what I ask.
Charity is ever
        Warmer when the brats
And their parents shiver,
        Like half-drowned rats.
                Oh, the joys of cadging,
                Wife and kids at heels,
                No one can imagine
                Save the bloke that feels.'

Another section of the Ins and Outs is composed of professional thieves. These are fellows at the bottom of their profession, as a rule—low footpads who waylay children, and rob them of their school-pence—who snatch articles from passing carts, or who raid on street-stalls or on the displays in front of shops. Such fellows take to the house from various motives.

Now and again they come in to get out of the way of the police, and remain until a hint is conveyed to them that the coast is clear, and search after them discontinued. Still more frequently, however, they enter because 'work' has become very bad with them.

The last sentence requires a little explanation. Thieves of the kind I mention haunt the same localities, from the beginning of their career to the end. Their women and chums all tenant the quarter. It contains their favourite taps; and it is the beat of officers with whom they are familiar, and whom they know how to 'square' or avoid in cases of emergency. Moreover, they are hand and glove with all its fences, and are perfectly acquainted, as it were by instinct, with all its usages.

They have grown up in the locality, in short, and have been accustomed to it from their cradle; otherwise they would be but the tamest of bunglers even here. The intellect of these fellows is inconceivably mean. Tested in matters beyond those to which they have been habituated, they will be found utterly incapable of grasping them.

Such miserable practitioners must not migrate, and they know it. They would be completely at sea, as the phrase goes, anywhere save at home. In other places they would be under the necessity of acquiring new companions, securing new haunts, discovering new agents, and learning new usages. All these are difficulties which your intelligent depredator will master in a few days at most; but it would take the low-lived half a century to do so. He is perfectly aware of this, and therefore never migrates, save under the pressure of circumstances; and when he does so, it is invariably to be locked up in a very few hours.

The low-lived depredator, therefore, remains at home—in the quarter that he knows best, and where, as a thing of course, he himself is best known.

Cessation of business from time to time is as essential to this personage as to his victims, who are chiefly the tradesmen of the quarter. The latter very soon learn, to their cost, when one of these fellows is at large and at work, and naturally take measures for frustrating his efforts, or, better still, for trapping himself. It is then that times become hard with him; and if not caught and committed to prison at once, he betakes him to the workhouse for a period.

Of all the Ins and Outs, decidedly the most degraded are the men who subsist by fastening upon street-harlots and sharing their wretched earnings. They are all sturdy fellows, with a good deal of the pugilist, but much more of the sneak, in them—just the ones to bully a weakling or batter a drunken victim out of all recognition. When their mistresses come to grief and are placed under lock and key, which happens frequently, the 'fancy man' generally manages to skulk out of the mischief and escape scot-free. But as such a fellow never did an honest day's work in his life, and never means to, and as besides lie has no friends, but is contemned and shunned by even the thief who has any self-respect, he has nothing for it but to take shelter in the house while the woman remains a prisoner. He takes good care, however, to discharge himself so as to meet her at the prison-door on the morning of her release.

Ins and Outs of all sorts are agents of demoralisation, and nothing else, in a workhouse. Their chatter—and they are always chattering—is loose at all times, and infamous—often hideously infamous. It is never so wicked, however, as after they go to bed, and, the dormitory-doors being locked, the paupers are left to themselves for the night. Then hours upon hours are whiled away by themselves and their companions, the former in recounting vile stories, and the latter in marking, learning, and inwardly digesting what they hear.

Tiptop-spree men, mouchers, thieves, and bullies make many recruits, especially among the juniors. Nor can even the best disposed escape the contagion which these rascals carry with them. Their moral tone is lowered, in spite of themselves, by constant contact. There is no reproving these men without bringing a quarrel about one's ears, in which the reprover is pretty sure to stand alone against a score or more. There is sufficient provision, indeed, made for this kind of thing by Act of Parliament; but the clauses are never enforced. No officer will venture to enforce them spontaneously, and no pauper dare call upon him to enforce them. The blackguards thus have things all their own way; and even the most delicate ears must become callous at length, and the firmest principles damaged, through constant contact with unmitigated ribaldry.

In some respects the origin of the Ins and Outs may be readily explained. There are men here who fought against indoor pauperism at the outset, as though they were contending against death itself, and did not enter until they were at the last gasp. However, the plunge once made over the workhouse threshold, it effaced much of the fine feelings which stimulated them to abstain from taking shelter therein; and a stay of a few weeks within goes far towards effacing all the rest.

Suppose the man to go out soon afterwards and obtain employment, he may resume his place in society, but he is no longer the same individual. The next time difficulties arise, his thoughts naturally suggest the workhouse as the best refuge. He has little shame to deter him from entering it this time, and manifests small reluctance in doing so. It is easier, he finds, to become an indoor pauper than to undergo privations and hardships. So it goes on with him. On each fresh occasion he goes to the relieving officer with smaller cause than before, until, ere long, he becomes a confirmed and hopeless In and Out.

Chapter V.
Fun In The House.

A PUBLIC school is a rare place for broad fun and practical joking; so is a barrack-room, or the 'tween-decks of a troopship. But these are all far surpassed, in fun and frolic, by the young men's side of the particular workhouse of which I happen to be a tenant.

There are several causes for this superiority of the pauper in matters farcical. In the first place, the materials thereof are far more varied and better adapted for producing comic effect than elsewhere. In the second place, the active agents of humour are keener and more expert at the work. And in the third place, practical joking and playing upon the foibles of neighbours is by far the most inviting—indeed, almost the sole amusement of indoor paupers.

As comic subjects, indoor paupers may be divided into several classes. There are the idiots, pure and simple; the semi-idiotic; the monomaniacs; the inordinately vain, who are also monomaniacs in their way; the irritable; and, finally, the unsophisticated, or people who have the use of all their senses, but in whom, because as being new to the house, some of their senses have not yet been developed up to the pauper standard. The last, it need hardly be said, are only temporary butts; and, probably on account of the probation which they undergo, very often ripen into the primest of such jokers themselves.

And here it may be as well to make a few observations anent the senses of paupers. These senses are not limited among them, nor, indeed, among men of any class, to the five by means of which the spirit communicates with things external. There are internal senses which are acted upon by means of the organs of perception; as the senses of the ludicrous, the pleasant, the beautiful, the terrible, etc.—prominent among the etceteras being the sense that we are being victimized or rendered a laughing-stock. This particular sense is one that remains quiescent in most people, or nearly so, under ordinary circumstances. However, it is one very soon trained into full maturity and activity when time and place cohere; and in no place are the developing influences stronger than in the workhouse.

We have three or four idiots among us, each of whom displays, when roused, strongly marked peculiarities of temper; and it is a common amusement of the jokers to excite the idiotic temper as often as possible. Good opportunities present themselves four or five times a day. First, in the morning, during the half-hour intervening between rising and breakfast. When the laggards descend from their dormitories, they are sure .to find the idiots, each in his own corner, begirt by a troop of laughing tormentors, and growling, storming, and swearing, it may be, each in his own peculiar manner.

To the credit of the jesters, it must be told that they prefer to play upon the milder peculiarities of the idiots, and make them ridiculous by dwelling upon and drawing out their predominant likings.

Similar scenes are to be witnessed before each of the other meals; but, to see them in full perfection, one must tenant a dormitory wherein sleeps an idiot—or, better, two or three. Here they are played upon by masterly performers, and drawn into perpetrating all sorts of ridiculous acts, to the high satisfaction of everybody about them, and in most cases very much to their own.

The semi-idiotic belong, for the most part, to the lowest class of Ins and Outs. They are fellows accustomed to draw the laughter of tap-room boozers, and with it their contributions, in the shape of half-pints of small-beer and odd coppers, quite as much by submitting with docility to the practical jokes as by their own amusing qualities. They have been in the habit, indeed, of playing tomfool so long, that the part has become natural, and adheres to them at all times.

These fellows are the delight of the workshops in the absence of the labour-masters. The moment these officials turn their backs, one or other of the semi-idiots is called upon to give a specimen of his comic powers, or to relate some laughable incident of his own experiences. Generally the call is responded to willingly, and we have tumbling, singing, and acting—the last of a sort that would astonish Mr. Henry Irving very considerably. If the fellow refuses to gratify his mates, he is jeered at and goaded until he accedes, or flies off into a towering passion—the latter invariably affording his tormentors much more entertainment than any other performance of his.

Perhaps the foremost of our semi-idiots is Jack Queedom a local notoriety outside the house as well as inside. He is one of the shortest specimens of manhood among us, with a curious monkey sort of phiz, and a figure and a gait tending to excite risibility at first sight. The voice is one to match—a long-drawn nasal howl which never varies its dreary tone in the least.

Jack is renowned for his Shakespearean recitations, which must have been taught him by a master-wag. He muddles up about a dozen choice speeches into a single rigmarole; and he gives new readings of the more remarkable passages, which render them beyond measure comical. At the same time, he is perfectly unconscious that he is doing anything of the kind, believing most firmly that he is adhering exactly to the text, when he makes his most curious departures from it; as, for instance, when, in the character of Richard III., he orders Buckingham's head to be put upon a plate instead of on a pole.

The most conspicuous traits in the character of this worthy are his extreme credulity, on the one side, and his capacity as extreme for recounting every incident of his life exactly as it occurred, omitting not a single item, no matter how ridiculous it makes him appear.

His most amusing stories are those which concern his adventures with the women, of whom Jack is a devoted admirer. There are few low-class females dwelling adjacent to the house who are not acquainted with Jack and all his weaknesses, and very few indeed who are not ready to take advantage of them.

Somehow, when he goes out, lie can always manage to raise a few shillings; and these the beauties of his acquaintance know how to melt,' as fast as he obtains them. It is, however, of the past that his best anecdotes of dealing with women are told. He really was once a steady workman, in constant employment; and then Jack Queedom, from Saturday night to Monday morning, was the inevitable victim of the queans.

He has been tarred, though not feathered, covered with flour and red-ochre, physicked too, and lie has suffered other inflictions of the like sort innumerable at their hands. He has even been befooled into handing over to one and another of them, from time to time, the fees indispensable for putting up the 'askings' or banns; but, without exception, the fair one has transferred the coins to the favourite tavern-keeper, in return for the adequate number of pots of four ale, to be consumed by herself and her acquaintances.

All this Jack tells us most artlessly, but withal so comically as to keep everybody in a roar. And when the tale is told, it is made the medium of badgering him until he loses all command of himself, and, rushing off to the labour-master, lie forswears all further work for that day, and demands to be locked up in the refractory ward—purely to escape from his tormentors. His request, I need hardly remark, is always granted. And there he remains until bedtime.

Pestered and plagued, however, as he is, Jack Queedom is quite a favourite in the house. His temporary absences are loudly lamented, so long as they last; and his returns are always hailed with acclamation. The house, it is generally allowed, would be nothing without him; and it may be added that he, in his turn, would be nothing without the house.

Next to the Queedoms come the monomaniacs; and chief among these is the one known as General Booth.' Left to himself, the man is quiet and silent enough, reserved and retiring—very much so indeed. But when turned on,' as the phrase goes here, he bursts out into a roar, reciting a series of hymns and passages of Scripture mixed up with canting ejaculations. He utters these pious scraps in exactly the same order on all occasions. He never omits a single sentence, or introduces anything fresh. It is the same, without the smallest variation even of tone, from one end of the day to the other.

The worst of it is, there is no stopping the fellow once he begins. He is bound to go on until the excitement subsides, and that often takes hours. At first his roar is a subject of laughter; but ten minutes or so of it is certain to disgust the most inveterate Jack-joker of the lot. Then he is roared at and execrated on all sides, but without the smallest effect. Those who have provoked the infliction—and it is but right to state that it is, as a rule, provoked, and that very often much time and ingenuity is required to compel the poor fellow into giving tongue—those who have provoked the infliction, I repeat, are bound to put up with it until the speaker is run dry.

Of course there is no fun in the man himself; or in his rhapsody; but there is a good deal in the suddenness with which it breaks forth, in its contrast to what is going on, in its ear-splitting strength, and in the vigour with which it is persisted in, notwithstanding oaths and threats of the most astounding order.

Far more amusing than the monomaniacs are the men each of whom is cursed with a pet vanity, of whom we have a number. This one, for instance, is an unrivalled scholar—in his own view; that one, a profound philosopher; a third is an orator or tragedian; a fourth, a theologian—and so on. These people are always to be got at by deferential wheedling and adroit flattery; and when got at, the victim of the moment shows off in high exulting style, until finally brought to a sudden halt by an uproarious outburst of laughter. Then come sneer, and jeer, and mockery anent the subject of his discourse, and especially the principal subject himself, until the poor fellow loses his temper and behaves accordingly—which is considered the climax of the joke.

Joe Collier is far and away the most conspicuous of our vanity-mongers. He is a little elderly man, with boyish features but stentorian voice; and his delight is to expatiate on the 'points' of the countless beauties of all lands who have wasted their affections upon him.

Joe is one of our occasionals; that is, he will stick to the house for a couple of months, and then vanish from it for four, five, or six, and always as accepting legitimate occupation. He is sure, however, to return, greatly to the satisfaction of the inmates who have already made his acquaintance.

How he entered the house at the outset is more than I know; but, once in it, he contrived to fall in love with the cook—a woman on the wrong side of fifty, who, moreover, remains to this hour in perfect ignorance of the impression made by her on Joe's susceptible heart. He flattered himself, of course, that she had fallen in love with him; and the rogues in his confidence used to make a good thing of forging letters and messages in her name, and bearing them to Joe during their outings,' when the poor fellow happened to be in employment.

Joe's tirades are exceedingly popular. They are all of the high falutin' style, anent Circassian beauties, golden hair, jetty locks, laughing eyes, glowing cheeks, sylph-like figures, and the rest of it. And decked as they are with luscious stories, which do credit to Joe's imagination, if not to his taste or morals, they go down excellently. The rascals round listen with delight, especially to the luscious stories, putting sly questions now and again to draw Joe still further, and always with the desired effect.

While the tales last—that is, so long as Joe's lungs can hold forth—all goes well. But the moment he 'dries up,' or ceases to speak, the listeners cast aside their deferential demeanour, and the badgering commences, and goes on, too, until Joe starts up in a rage and 'pitches into' the nearest of his tormentors.

Then begins a battle, which is only make-believe on one side, and which is so conducted as to extract thunders of applause from the spectators. Joe strikes out wildly, while his antagonist shifts and dodges in ludicrous fashion, now and again pretending to be badly hurt, but still more frequently laying Joe on his back in all sorts of queer ways, though without hurting him in the least. And so the thing goes on until some one on the watch cries, Nix lads, buttons l'—the warning that the taskmaster is at hand. Then the row ceases, everybody takes his seat and resumes his work, and the most consummate order meets the eye of the official when he enters the apartment.

A good deal of fun is knocked out of the hobbledehoys from sixteen to nineteen, half a dozen or more of whom are always about, and who, having spent most of their time in the workhouse, are singularly ignorant of many matters of the commonest sort, and therefore to be gulled with the greatest ease respecting them.

One of these youths, having a grievance against the parish doctor, was persuaded by a scamp to travel to the Isle of Wight, in order to state his complaint to the Queen in person, as being the proper person to do him right in the matter; and the lad actually took his discharge and travelled down to Portsmouth, supporting himself on the way by begging and sheltering at night in casual wards, with this silly purpose and no other; nor was he disabused, until he tried to persuade the master of a steamer to carry him across the Solent.

Much fun, too, is made by conveying false orders to simpletons in the name of various officers, and so setting them to work on tasks which no sensible man would dream of assigning them. Thus a booby has been made to mount a tolerable-sized pig on his shoulders, and carry it to the doctor for his opinion concerning some imaginary complaint which the jokers assigned to the animal.

The fun, however, of the males is strictly confined to the young men's side of the house: there is nothing of the sort among the old men. The latter, indeed, taken as a whole, are about the most irritable and cross-grained beings in existence. They are perpetually on the watch for the slightest invasion of what they consider 'their rights,' and as perpetually vindicating the said rights by growl and snarl and venomous remark. To listen to them one would think that they were for ever on the point of coming to blows.

Poor fellow! All things considered, their snarling is more to be pitied than blamed. There is no hope for them of escape from the house and its miserable existence. There is ample reason why, therefore, all the acidity of their tempers should be for ever on the surface.

Chapter VI.
Love In The House.

It is my firm conviction that there is no English institution of which the public in general know less than of the workhouse. Most people look upon it as ruled by stupid guardians and unamiable, not to say dishonest, officials, and as the scene of endless peculation, oppression, and misery. But, as I think this small volume will show, the truth is much broader.

There are, of course, pig-headed guardians and unscrupulous officials in existence—far too many, I am afraid; but my own experience is that they do not form the majority of the bodies to which they belong. I go even further, and assert that much of the evil with which the one and the other are charged is absolutely forced upon them. Circumstances—the demands of constituents and the tenour of certain statutes as interpreted by certain authorities—have much workhouse mischief to answer for. Further—and it ought to be far more widely known than it is— there is a great deal in the character and habits of certain classes of indoor paupers to try the temper of guardians and officers, and to develop what is worst in their nature.

As to the workhouse itself, let it be always understood that it forms a world in itself. It has its factions and its demagogues, its intrigues and its animosities, and—stranger still, as no doubt outsiders will think—*its flirtations*. Moreover, the last deepen very frequently into fervid passion, and actually culminate, in a number of cases, in elopements.

True, as a rule, the runaways seldom disappear for ever. On the contrary, most of them return, often in a day or two. Still, indoor paupers really do elope, and for love, in pairs from time to time. Moreover, such events are just as eagerly canvassed within the limits of the house as things of the like sort outside.

All this, however, is only natural. People do not abandon humanity on quitting society for the workhouse. They do not subside into senseless clods on crossing its threshold, nor yet become animated but utterly passionless dolls. They do not, and cannot, lead the stagnant life in their seclusion that is commonly supposed. A little reflection will show all this.

At the same time, indoor paupers are free from a good many things which occupy a large share of the time and attention of persons elsewhere. They are free from pecuniary troubles, and from worrying anticipations concerning the morrow. They have no family cares, either, left to assail them. Food, shelter, and clothing for themselves, and for their children, too, if they have any, with a fair education and a fair start in life for the latter, are certainties, come what may, so far as they are concerned.

Meanwhile, their position secures them from a number of influences very powerful in the world beyond. State matters, with their negotiations and wars, the vicissitudes of commerce, the conflicts of parties, the burning questions and equally burning scandals of the hour, seldom weigh with them, or indeed reach them at all. In short, all the interests and sympathies of indoor paupers are concentrated within the house. In consequence, their friendships, hatreds, and notably their squabbles, assume an intensity which, considering the quality of the matters at issue, is simply ludicrous to the mere observer.

The loves of the workhouse, it needs hardly be said, are of a peculiar order. Contrary to what obtains elsewhere in the passion, the females with us are the active and aggressive agents; and for this there is very sufficient cause.

It is a fact that women are much more subject to abandon their individuality and bow to the influence of a stronger mind, when congregated in masses, than men. It is also a fact that, with women of the lower classes, the stronger-minded are almost exclusively those who have graduated in vicious practices. You will find it so in all those factories which give coarse employment to large numbers of females. Go into one of the workrooms of such a factory and examine for yourself. If you do, I am sure you will agree with me that, whatever they may have been originally, every one of the workers, except perhaps a few of the rawest, has gone down in language and sentiment, if not in conduct, to the level of the very lowest among them. Indeed, it is the very coarse females of the jam-factory, the match-factory, the jute-factory, etc., which give the tone and lay down the law as to demeanour, language, and action to their fellows. Depravity carries it over modesty in all such places; and depravity carries it among the females of the workhouse also.

Let me turn aside and examine for a moment how the female population of a workhouse is made up; of what materials it is chiefly composed.

First come the young women with illegitimate children, who, having been compelled to resort to the house in the first confinement, are sure to renew their acquaintance with it again and again on the like errand. Their experience of the house, indeed, encourages them. They are incomparably better cared for in their trouble than they would be elsewhere. And they fall at once into companionship that suits their situation exactly. There are no weeping mothers or sisters to reproach, and no indignant fathers or brothers to go somewhat beyond reproach. There are no former acquaintances to look at them askance, no prudes to preach to them officiously and mercilessly, and no sneering and jeering gossips to be dreaded. They are surrounded by women who have done the like or worse, and who, therefore, are the last persons in the world to throw verbal missiles at them.

A young woman who has gone astray, and who keeps aloof from the workhouse during her first confinement, may endure bitter hardships elsewhere, but she is far less likely to repeat the false step than her sister in misfortune who adopts the opposite course. Indeed, the chances are that the latter will continue to take false step after false step, if she does not plunge headlong into the streets at an early date, until she becomes overburdened with illegitimates, and so is compelled to enter the house as a permanent resident.

Even more complete and dangerous hussies than the fore going are the mistresses of habitual depredators, who become

60

indoor paupers whenever the paramours of the moment happen to be locked up and there are no other lovers at hand to take their places. These women, I need hardly remark, are those to whom the term 'fancy' specially applies.

That same term fancy,' I hope I may be allowed to remark, though very slangy and objectionable, is merely a corruption of the French *fiancée*, and has degenerated to its present use as follows:

In very old days, when wars between neighbouring lands were incessant, and when, therefore, border lands were dangerous places of residence and thinly tenanted, the spiritual wants of such residents were not to be ministered to without much trouble, and occasional peril, by the clergy. On both sides of the Cheviots, for instance, no church could be expected to stand for six months at a time, as being sure to be turned into a fortress during raids, and therefore equally sure to be attacked and destroyed by the raiders. There were no resident priests in such quarters, in consequence.

Once a year a clergyman, called a 'book bosom' from carrying the ritual in his breast, went round the district in order to marry and baptize those who needed. People, however, did not defer cohabitation, in all or even in the majority of cases, until the priest appeared. It was the custom for a pair who thought they suited one another to begin housekeeping on the understanding that they were to remain together for a year and a day, which was about the longest term that could intervene between the visits of the clergyman. If they liked one another as well when he appeared as before, they were wedded at once; if not, they parted. The probationary union was termed living *fiancée*. Whence the 'living fancy' of slang.

A 'fancy' woman then is several removes from a common harlot, and values herself on her superiority. It is her boast that she consorts with but one man—*at a time*. But it is also her boast that she refuses to be tied to a single one for her lifetime, or, indeed, for one moment longer than her inclination lasts. The lover of the moment is always the 'best' man within her reach. Should another and, in her estimation, a better man become accessible, she will incontinently abandon the other for him, and consider herself perfectly justified in doing so.

The paramour of the professional thief, it may be as well to remark, hardly ever has children, which is, perhaps, the chief cause of her fickleness. But she looks upon herself in all respects as a wife while 'engaged,' and, in most cases, behaves as such.

The mother of successive illegitimates is of another sort. She is usually self-supporting—a tailoress or factory hand, given to different flirtations every night she goes out to enjoy' herself, and whose 'mishaps' are not the result of attachment to any particular man or men, but of a spree with a casual acquaintance—one, it may be, picked up at haphazard in the street and seen for the first and last time on that particular occasion.

In addition to such lost women as the foregoing, the workhouse opens its gates to others who have fallen somehow into the trick of, alternating spells of indoor pauper life with spells of common prostitution. This sort of existence is seldom commenced before the individual has attained her thirtieth year, and is usually suggested by experience of the place and its ways during a severe fit of illness, when, having neither friends nor means, and no other shelter, the poor creature was compelled to resort to the infirmary of the Union.

At first her spells in the streets are much longer than those in the house; but by degrees the former diminish, and the latter lengthen, until, by the time she reaches her fortieth year, she limits her street life to two or three days a month. When such a woman discharges herself, she makes not the smallest secret of her purpose. The thing, and the probabilities thereof, are discussed by herself and her ward and workshop acquaintances in all their details. Guardians and officers are aware of it, too, but they are powerless to prevent. Now and again, an inexperienced chairman will take such a hussy to task; but, as a rule, to get the worse in the encounter. She is dead sure, when challenged with quitting the house for an immoral purpose,' not only to acknowledge the fact, but to exult in it; and, while justifying it, she invariably contrives to make a laughingstock of her assailant. Nothing can exceed the outrageous cynicism of the remarks made by the culprit on these occasions.

They are sure to make the round of all the officers and inmates, and to remain fixtures on the memories of the latter at least.

All these women are alike—brazen and bullying, reckless and rollicking, glorying in their shame, or making a pretence of doing so. There is, however, much that is taking about them. They are what is called 'good hearted'—generous to those who come in their way when they have anything to give, and ready to render any little service in their power to whoever needs. Their tongues are for ever in motion; and they are always heard with rapt attention. They are replete with pungent anecdotes of the lascivious order, and they never weary of narrating the fun and frolic of their experiences.

At the same time, these fallen creatures never miss an opportunity of sneering at the virtues, notably the one virtue in which they are themselves so conspicuously lacking. According to them, all women whatsoever are alike in inclination from the moment they cease to be children. According to them, too, the vast majority of women are exactly alike in conduct, the only difference between those of modest repute and themselves consisting in this—that the former have not yet been found out. They will have it, indeed, that modest women are merely consummate hypocrites, and therefore much worse than themselves, since they add this vice—the most detestable of all in the speaker's eye—to the rest.

Placed, as they are, among a number of young wives and growing girls, the influence for evil of the termagants cannot be overrated; for the said wives and girls, be it carefully noted, are just in the mood to drink in their detestable lessons. Taking the former all round, or in the bunch,' as themselves would put it, they have none of them any great cause for entertaining strong affection for the husbands who have fixed them where they find themselves—in a position where it is impossible to enjoy that life which was given them chiefly to be enjoyed, and this, too, at its most enjoyable season. Why should they? But this is a subject remarked upon elsewhere in this volume.

As to the very young girls, who are no longer children, they are shut out from all that intercourse with the other sex which is a necessity of their nature, and which, under judicious direction, is the very best teacher of true modesty. Their strong but uncultured instincts turn eagerly to the conversation of the fallen women, and luxuriate in every sentence. Thus they become utterly depraved in sentiment before they are afforded an opportunity of entering the world. How can young wives subjected to such an ordeal retain a due regard for the marriage contract? How can young girls similarly dealt with ever entertain any such regard at all?

With all her stronger feelings seconding the precepts of the temptresses, the young indoor-pauper wife is not long in coming to the conclusion that they are quite in the right as to manners and morals, while she herself has been, so far, altogether in the wrong. In short, she adopts their principles in the bulk, and longs for an opportunity of reducing them to practice. Nor in many instances is the opportunity long withheld.

Now and again the professional procuress makes her appearance in the house as an indoor pauper, and mostly finds the minds of the women, married and single, who suit her best, ready moulded to her hand. She has no difficulty at all in enlisting them; and seldom finds any in procuring their release. She may posture as a friend of the family, and so tempt her out into the world, or procure somebody else to do the trick. And out again in the world the discontented wife is sure to disappear, with the 'family friend,' at an early date, leaving husband and children to return to the workhouse at their leisure. It needs hardly be remarked that the work of the procuress is still easier with the very young girl.

But, even without the aid of the procuress, the fate of the young girl is determined in the very worst way. Sooner or later she is sure to be tempted into the streets by one of the harlots, and, a certain age attained, there is nothing to prevent. However, these are matters with which I have not now to deal. My immediate subject is love in the workhouse' itself—love among indoor paupers; and it is time to explain how it can possibly take place—in other words, how indoor paupers of different sexes are brought in contact.

Nearly all the work of the house is done by inmates—the women taking the laundry, the sewing, the mending, and other feminine occupations, and the men the whitewashing, painting, etc. Obviously a good deal of intercourse must take place between males and females while these matters are in progress.

Again, in nearly every instance, the officers are mere over-lookers and preservers of order. The real work of their posts is performed by pauper deputies, who are thus carried all over the house every day in the week. Necessarily these underlings must have the full use of their faculties in order to be efficient. In other words, they must not yet be 'old.' Moreover, they must be selected from the best material in the house; and human beings whose prime is not yet past, and who are pent in from year's end to year's end from the outer world, cannot meet, even for a few seconds, without plunging up to the eyes in flirtation. Both sides, indeed, are eager for it. In consequence, more progress in an intrigue is made in five minutes, by a pair of indoor paupers when they happen to meet, than is made in as many weeks by persons more fortunately placed.

A couple of meetings will suffice to engage a pair. And once the engagement is: formed, the parties to it must have frequent communication, and all sorts of tricks and contrivances are employed to secure it. Confidants on both sides are indispensable, and found without difficulty. All other paupers, indeed, make it a point of honour to further such an affair. Messages are exchanged; so are little notes, most of which are curiosities in their way. Many are penned on the margins of old newspapers, in the queerest possible hands, and in such spelling as is scarcely to be met with elsewhere. I have seen a pauper love-letter scratched with a nail on the bowl of an old iron spoon.

Flirtations among paupers on very rare occasions end as elsewhere, in marriage; and such marriages, when they do take place, are not so unhappy in result as might be supposed. They tempt the parties into making a vigorous and therefore successful effort at independence.

As a rule, however, a pauper flirtation is evanescent—a matter of six weeks or two months. Within that time it attains full intensity. Then—no better means presenting itself—the enamoured pair discharge themselves on the same morning, and go out to spend twelve to forty-eight hours together, according to the amount of money at their disposal. This is at once the consummation of the love-fit and its close. They resume their places in the house completely cured of it.

Small officials in a workhouse are the principal offenders in this way; these, it may be as well to remember, have always at their command the means of accumulating five or six shillings in, say, half as many months, halfpenny by halfpenny, by means described elsewhere.

All this is very immoral; but how, I must ask, is it to be prevented? Neither officers nor guardians have the power. The thing goes on day after day, and week after week, under their very eyes; but they cannot interfere, even though it may end now and again in the way most exasperating to right-minded guardians, by bringing additional burdens on the ratepayers.

In London workhouses, the hopping season is the grand opportunity of their more inveterate pauper flirts. Numbers of them go regularly to the hop-gardens; and each man must have a female companion—a hopping wife,' as she is termed—selected from the females on the other side. As I write (middle of August), not less than a dozen negotiations tending in this direction are in progress, literally within earshot.

Guardians encourage such excursions, because they relieve the rates to a marked extent while they last; though I question if they would be quite so ready to facilitate them as they often are, did they realise their full meaning. Not a few curious incidents take place during these hopping honeymoons. The fidelity of the women is never to be relied on. In the greater number of instances, indeed, they change partners on the ground, and return to London in company with the favoured lovers, who as often as not have been, and will be again in a day or two, inmates of the same workhouse as the original lovers.

The feuds that result between the rivals are sure to be lasting, and equally sure to furnish the house with abundant amusement. But enough of this.

CHAPTER VII.
OLD AND YOUNG.

THERE are two classes of indoor paupers who are much to be pitied—the very old and the young. The former have to drone away life in dullest monotony, half fed and little cared for. With the exception of a few in such manifest debility that even the most cruel-hearted would scarcely think of demanding labour from them, they are all turned into the workshops, given their task, and kept at it just as long as the men are in full vigour.

There is a curious rule as to old and young. An advanced age is laid down, up to the attainment of which the person is considered a young man,' and subject to all the conditions imposed on that class of pauper.

The same rule obtains, I believe, in the prisons; but there it is invariable. Up to the conclusion of his sixtieth year a convict is a young man. He remains so until he completes the three hundred and sixty-fifth day of the said sixtieth year and passes the sixtieth anniversary of his birthday. Up to that moment he must take his spell at the crank, or any other toil known as 'hard labour,' But the instant he enters his sixty-first year he becomes 'old,' and his hard labour ceases at a stroke.

It is just the same in the workhouse, with the exception that the line between youth and old age is not laid down exactly at the same period in all these places. In none of them, let it be observed, is it under sixty; while in many it is placed as much over sixty and as close to seventy as the guardians care—I had almost written *dare*—to put it.

I should like to know why this is done. I cannot see any special reason. The task-work of the most vigorous is not very profitable. And it is impossible to get more labour out of an old man than his muscles can accomplish. One species of task-work, I have been informed—oakum-picking—is either a dead loss, or very little better—so little better, indeed, that the toil of the most skilful and industrious, one day with another, is never worth more to the guardians than a single penny at most.

As to other matters, the old man is supposed to receive better food than the young man, and to enjoy a number of little privileges denied to the latter. But does he?

I learn from the public journals that the food of the indoor pauper differs much according to the locality, and that the difference is in exact proportion to the quality of the guardians. I saw, the other day, the report of an exulting comparison on this particular point, made at the sitting of a certain Board by the clerk. He pointed out that while the average cost of feeding and clothing *his* paupers was three shillings a head, the cost in neighbouring Unions which he named never fell below that amount, while in most instances it ran much higher. His was a district abounding in retail traders, it may be as well to state, while the other districts rose in the quality of the guardians just as the cost of keeping the pauper advanced, that in which the guardians were most aristocratic being about twice as generous to the pauper prisoner as that in which the guardians were all retail traders. The fact is significant.

Now my own workhouse is ruled exclusively by retail traders, and persons, as doctors, who may be considered at their mercy. The retail trader, indeed, has it all his own way here; and that way is certainly not a pleasant one for the indoor pauper. I do not know how the items stand in the official balance-sheet, but I am very certain of one thing—that the average cost of keeping a young-man indoor pauper, setting aside, as aforesaid, the necessary expenses of the establishment, does not exceed two shillings a week—if it ever reaches that sum—of which I have my doubts. The dietary scale has been revised and re-revised with us until it has been brought down to starvation point. It is at the lowest that can be reached, and will admit of no further retail revision.

One result of this peculiar economy is actually to swell the rates. When a muscular man comes into the house, he is absolutely tortured by hunger for three weeks or a month. At the end of that time, if he remain so long, the ravenous craving ceases. This is because his stomach has adapted itself to the regimen; and this in its turn comes from the fact that the muscles have contracted as far as contraction is possible, and no longer require their normal supply of nutriment. But mark the consequences.

The semi-skeleton—for such the man now is—receives a hint from friends outside that times have improved; that there is a demand for hands in his own line; that, in short, employment is awaiting him. He discharges himself and goes out to it accordingly. But, in half an hour or so, he discovers that he is no longer the same man that he used to be, and is not up to his work. His mates discover it too, and, unless he happens to be popular among them, they begin to grumble at having more than their fair share of the labour thrust upon them through he is either discharged; or he gives up the job; or he meets his bodily weakness. One of three things then happens: with an accident. In the two former cases he is 'booked' once more for the workhouse; and in the latter also, unless he happens to be killed outright. This is the general rule. As to exceptions, it requires more than average popularity among masters and mates, and more than average resolution, too, for a man fresh from the workhouse to stick to his work until he has fed himself up to his former strength.

The young man in the workhouse does not get enough to eat by a great deal, and the old man gets less. He is allowed tea, indeed, butter, and one or two other things denied to his juniors, and meat more frequently—*in some houses*. But the quantity? That question is best answered by stating the simple fact that I have known old men' beg and pray to be restored to the 'young men's' scale of dietary, and to congratulate themselves when the request was granted, and for no other reason than because they had a better chance of filling their stomachs thereby.

As to other matters, an old man cannot enjoy his tea unless he be provided somehow with sugar from the outside. Against this fact I am bound to set another: the scullery-men will always sell a pauper a basin of tea. By such sales, indeed, they contrive to realise sums considerable for paupers. The tea thus sold, it is right to state, is invariably much better than the house tea, and properly sweetened into the bargain. It is one of the 'perquisites' of the scullery-men, though why they should be allowed the privilege of fleecing their fellows—to say nothing of the stores— passes my comprehension. They are invariably the laziest men and most inveterate paupers in the house; but this has been dwelt upon elsewhere.

Elderly workhouse inmates.

Old men frequently die in their beds without having been removed to the infirmary, and unnoted of their fellows. They are found dead in the morning; that is all. This brings me to the mention of a curious fact in connection with this particular establishment. It was opened with the fewest possible appliances at the outset. Things absolutely necessary were omitted in order to curtail the cost. Inquest after inquest have compelled the guardians, much against the grain, to supply several of these things. For instance, one inquest on an indoor pauper brought about the introduction of lights of an evening into certain passages. And another inquest, which came off only the other day, compelled the guardians, for the first time, to place night-lamps in the dormitories.

A number of other essentials are still wanting; and they will be supplied, no doubt, in response to the demands of future coroners and their juries, *but not otherwise.*

As regards the young—I mean the very young, the lads between sixteen and twenty—I say that they should never be allowed to mix for even a moment with the more mature. I have given good reasons elsewhere, especially in the chapter on Pauper Vices. I say further that, properly treated, they would be the most hopeful section of the community to which they belong, while, as things go, they are positively the most hopeless. They are trained in all that is degrading—in skulking, in laziness, in lying, in impudence, in the vilest habits. No alternative, indeed, is left them between the life of the pauper and that of the criminal. They must choose between; and generally they elect to become both. It is heart-sickening to see such youths, and that, too, by the score and the hundred, undergoing ruin in every sense of the word, strictly *according to law.*

They learn no craft—I speak of lads in this particular workhouse: they pick oakum and break stones, and can do both skilfully. But neither accomplishment, I submit, can gain them an honest living outside. The only real use of either, indeed, is to deprive the gaol of its principal terrors, so far as the pauper youth is concerned. 'Hard labour,' pronounced by judge or magistrate, does not trouble him in the least. 'He can do that on his head,' as he seldom fails to inform the *Beak* who awards his sentence.

But even this is not the worst of it. There is *malingering*—a habit once only too well known in the British army. It consisted in self-mutilation by a skulker in order to secure an easy life in hospital, or, if need were, discharge. There are plenty of ex-malingerers in the workhouse; and these fellows never fail to instruct the youths round them in the secrets of their craft, and concerning the times and circumstances when they may be used with striking effects. They are used, too, and the results brought forward, first in the workhouse and then in the prison, to procure immunity from the more trying tasks and the more severe punishments.

Youth under twenty are, I find, beginning to abound in the metropolitan workhouses, for a reason which is a sign of the times, and a very sad sign. Parents of the lowest class, who have a son among their children too weak in body or mind, or both, to succeed in life as artisan or labourer, are in the habit of turning him out of doors when he attains his sixteenth year. As a rule he is previously made thoroughly well acquainted with his infirmities, and the lot they are certain to entail upon him, and he is taught to look upon the workhouse as his only home, and that, too, a much more comfortable one than he has been accustomed to. A story also is put into his mouth, and precautions are taken to support it, should the relieving officer call to inquire. Then he is represented as a waif, an orphan, turned out of doors by an unfeeling stepfather; and thus he is made an indoor pauper. A similar course, I need hardly say, is pursued with girls in the like case; but of these I know little.

I have, however, met with a number of workhouse youths, soon to be workhouse men, whose parents and brothers and sisters are in comfortable circumstances—nay, comparatively affluent.

This is an age of organized benevolence—of charity done systematically by the medium of paid agents. It seems to me that this charity and these agents could not be better employed than in giving some attention and judicious aid to workhouse youths ere they become too hardened in workhouse ways and vices.

CHAPTER VIII.
SATURDAY NIGHT IN THE DORMITORY.

Saturday night, for various reasons, is a lively night in our workhouse dormitories. It is the close of the week here as well as elsewhere, and the morrow is a day of rest, with an additional hour in bed. Therefore the younger men, at least, are disposed to lie awake longer on that night and amuse themselves somehow or other. Then there is old habit. Saturday night, in better times, was public-house and concert-hall night—general roystering night, in short. And the indoor pauper cannot so far forget old habit, and is not so utterly broken down in spirits, as not to attempt to 'keep it up,' and do a little roystering even here.

Up we go to the dormitories at a quarter to eight. Ten minutes or so are occupied in changing under-clothing and getting between the sheets. The labour-master goes his round and sees that all is right. By a quarter-past eight at latest all doors are locked, and all lights, save that of the recently introduced night-lamps, extinguished, and the men are left to themselves for eleven long hours.

There is a good deal of desultory chat between the occupants of adjoining beds, who are always more intimate than the rest—comrades, in fact. This, however, soon drops. Then comes a voice, belonging to one of the influential personages in the room, calling 'Order—order!'

Order it is in an instant—a pin-drop silence, in fact. This obtained, the influential personage requests in his politest manner—and he can be very courteous when it pleases him—Mr. Nameless to oblige the company with the story of one of his innumerable thrilling adventures.

Mr. Nameless is a white-haired man, rather under the middle height, spare of figure, but broad-shouldered and long in the arm, with an erect form and a firm elastic tread. His face is frank and open, and his dark eye remarkably brilliant. As a rule he is reserved; and just as quiet. But when roused by gratuitous insult, or gross attempts at imposition—things both rather too common in this workhouse of ours—he is pronounced by those who have witnessed his method of resenting such things a *very demon*.

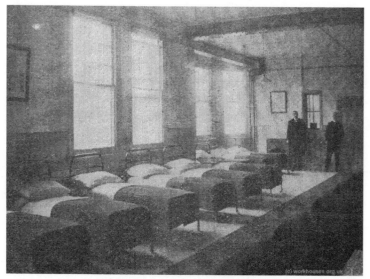

A London workhouse dormitory.

'He can use his fists, sir,' remarked an informant, 'as well as Jem Mace himself, is a first-rate wrestler, and tough as steel into the bargain. Therefore the biggest blackguard in the house fights shy of him, as far too awkward a customer to play tricks upon.

'And who and what is he?' I inquired.

'Nobody can answer those questions but himself,' was the reply. 'But I would not myself like- to be the man to put them, nor would I advise anybody else to do so either. One or two things, however, I can tell you. He knows every mortal thing that man can know, and he's been all over the world; at least, nobody could describe foreign scenes and peoples as he can, unless from personal observation; he speaks no end of languages, too, and keeps a Greek Testament and a copy of Dante at the head of his bed. He spends most of his leisure time in writing, though what it is all about none of us can guess. We have our suspicions, however, and not respecting his writing only. I shall not be surprised, myself, to find him missing any morning. It is my own private opinion that he is a Continental conspirator—a Nihilist, or something of that sort, who has come in here as the best place of hiding for a time.'

So much for what indoor paupers thought of the story-teller. As to the story itself, it is a vivid account of a tiger-hunt in Upper India. The speaker never uses the first person, but it is clear that he was an eye-witness of what he describes, moreover an actor in the affair. The incident is admirably told in a series of word-pictures. Evidently the man is an artist in narrative. The language and manner are equally choice—not a word too much, no slurring over interesting details, and not the smallest approach to wire-drawing.

How well he recounts is evinced in the breathless interest and hasty exclamations of the audience, who manifest almost as much emotion as if they were there and then taking part in a tiger-hunt.

The story occupies about half an hour, and is followed by a storm of applause, which again is succeeded by a number of eager questions respecting the 'sport' and the appliances used in it, which would be spun out to any extent, did not the influential personage interpose imperiously and forbid his comrades to worry 'the gentleman'—the story-teller's distinctive title—with any more of their 'stupid queries.'

Silence once again secured, somebody is called upon for a song. There is seldom any reluctance in acceding. The song over, the singer uses his privilege in calling upon somebody else. Now and again a recitation or an anecdote is accepted instead, but there are no more set stories. The 'gentleman' gives but one of a night, and after him the story-telling of anybody else were wearisome and unprofitable.

So far I have been writing of my own dormitory, which may be accepted as typical of all the rest; and to the end of this chapter I shall confine my description to the said dormitory. As it happens, it is tenanted by a number of choice singers, three or four of whom possess voices of musical harmony quite sufficient to secure their success as professionals; they are good fellows into the bargain. Conspicuous among them is my own particular acquaintance and next bedfellow on one side, 'the Pensioner,' of whom more in another place.

'Tune up, Mac!' calls out a fellow from the other end of the room.

'Yes, yes,' repeat a dozen voices. 'A song from Mac. Order for a song from Mac!'

'Well, I suppose I must,' replies Mac. 'A few more whiffs of the pipe, and I am ready.'

Mac, I must explain, has a habit, which is general, of smoking in bed; that is to say, when he happens to have any tobacco to smoke, which is not always. It is a habit, however which has never led to mischief, and—say the smokers—is never likely to lead to any. There are too many men in the room not to detect a fire in its incipient and harmless state, and prevent it from acquiring dangerous proportions.

'All right,' reply a dozen men together, 'we can wait; only don't be long.'

A few minutes of conversation follow while Mac finishes his smoke. Then he pulls his pipe from his mouth and clears his throat—a signal that he is ready. It is also a signal for silence, which is instantly obtained. Then my 'Pensioner' pours forth in a rich mellow voice, and in right good style, 'The Old Musqueteer.'

The song is received with enthusiasm. When the applause dies away, Mac exercises his right, and calls upon somebody else to aid in entertaining the company.

Somebody else, it is well known, *can* sing; but he either is, or pretends to be, out of voice, and recites with deep feeling Lord Ullin's Daughter instead. It takes almost as well as a song. Then the reciter calls upon our singer of singers—the Sims Reeves or Braham of the house, Jack Blades.

'Hear, hear!' respond all the rest; 'Jack Blades, Jack Blades! One with a chorus, Jack, one with a chorus;' and several of Jack's favourites are suggested. Jack, however, gives none of these.

Even before the last voice is silent, Jack commences one as yet unheard in the dormitory from his lips. Beginning low, almost in a whisper, but such a whisper 1—one heard distinctly in every corner of the room—jack's splendid baritone is heard rising higher and higher—piling note upon note, as it were, gathering power as it peals, until it develops into a perfect torrent of richest music; then it sails down the gamut in a lilt without words. All this by way of prelude

Everybody is now still as death. When the lilt ceases you may hear even the hearts around you beating. Not for more than five seconds, though. That short interval past, Jack bursts forth in a grand old sea song, with the right sort of chorus, commencing 'A long, long pull, and a strong, strong pull,' and does it ample justice. The splendid voice—for such it really is—absolutely fills the room with delicious sound. Better still, every word of the song is distinctly audible.

So one can fancy Incledon sang in his day. And with the same rapt delight as Incledon's listeners hung on his voice, so do we hang on Jack's.

But when he comes to the chorus—how am I to describe that? 'The long, long pull, and the strong, strong pull' is indeed given with a will, with a dash and a spirit which show how completely everybody has been carried away by Jack's lyric.

Another recitation is now given, but nobody seems to care for it. It is therefore the last attempted. Then an inmate of the heavy-swell order, who turns all his 'r's' into 'w's,' gives us a music-hall ditty. Every lengthy stanza is a monotonous rigmarole; but that is excused on account of the rattling, though somewhat vulgar, refrain.

Then our own particular rival in the singing line to Jack Blades is called upon, and responds willingly. He has a capital voice, a more than average knowledge of music, and a choice collection of songs. Jack out of the way, this man would be an easy first in this particular line. He gives 'Tom Bowling,' and gives it well—with a taste and feeling that would have satisfied Dibdin. Everybody relishes it exceedingly. But the chorus?

Unfortunately for the singer, Jack Blades joins in here—is bound to do so, in fact. All other voices are reduced to silence by the manifest contest that opens between these two. For a few seconds there is little to choose between them. Then, however, Blades lets his voice loose in all its vigour, and his rival is nowhere, his voice being drowned, swallowed up, rendered altogether imperceptible by the fascinating tones of the grander organ.

'Tom Bowling' is encored, and Jack Blades gives the closing verse as he alone can give it.

Next volunteers a lad from the country—a stolid, potato faced youth, with a round, thunderous voice which has very little music in it. The words, however, smacking of the cornfield and sheepfold, of the cottage and the farmyard, take amazingly. The song also has a chorus; and the latter is given with a verve which tells how thoroughly the men accept its sentiments. Their hearts are not all in the sere and yellow leaf; there is something green about them yet, indoor paupers though they be.

My other next-bedfellow, Jack Macey, is now called upon. We have a rare assortment of 'Jacks' in our dormitory, I may explain; and this particular Jack is probably the quietest and best conducted of the name among us. Not long ago he was an under-foreman in one of our largest iron factories, understanding his particular department thoroughly, as well he might, seeing that he had been brought up in it, and discharging his duties on all occasions to the satisfaction of his employers. He had, besides, a faculty of dealing with men which rendered him popular with all who worked with and under him. Macey was prosperous, and likely to remain so; for the firm which he served seemed sound as the Bank of England itself, and just as likely to last. However, a crash came, no less complete than unexpected, and Jack was sent adrift at a moment's notice, with some thousands more; and—here he is.

The man would be an acquisition to any firm working in iron. He is in the prime of life; he bears the highest character; he is thoroughly up to his work, and, I repeat—here he is.

Jack's song, 'Meet me by Moonlight alone,' is sung in a rather subdued but very suggestive way. He has evidently had a careful musical training, and a tolerable organ, too; but it is the unquestionable touch of personal feeling ringing in it that gives it its chief interest. Everybody understands that though Macey himself is with us, his memory is far away in the past; that every line of his song speaks to him of what will never be again for him. Nobody, however, attempts to utter the general sentiment. When Jack has completed his song—giving the last line with a very perceptible quiver of voice—he buries his head in his pillow, and nothing more is heard of him for the rest of the night. No need to remark on the reason why

. As if coming to the rescue of most of us who feel rather awkwardly, Jack Blades burst forth without a call in 'Black-eyed Susan,' which is hailed with rapturous applause. His rival follows suit with 'The Red, White, and Blue,' which is chorused to the height. The hearts of these indoor paupers, it is clear, are in the right place so far as old England is concerned, even though she has treated many of them hardly, and that, too, in the opinion of others as well as in their own.

A short interval of silence follows, a quarter to eleven booms slowly from the great clock, and then my friend, Mac, gives 'Auld Lang Syne' as he alone can give it, in the dialect of Burns, and in a manner that would have won the hearty approval of the poet.

Thus the entertainment of the indoor paupers' Saturday evening is wound up. There is a little more chat between individuals, but it soon dies away, and, in ten minutes more, everybody is asleep.

From beginning to end, not a single wanton joke has been attempted, and not a single licentious song has been sung. We

80

have been somewhat noisy, and considerably altogethery at times; but, in all other respects, we have kept well within the bounds of decorum. It is not that the dormitory is without its proportion of blackguards. The respectable men, however, predominate, and their weight of character represses the truculent and low-lived.

CHAPTER IX.
INDOOR PAUPER VICES.

FOREMOST among indoor pauper vices I take leave to place larceny. However, if all be true that we hear, the offence is far from being confined to them. There never yet was an establishment of any size or age in which abuses did not prevail, simply because no system of management can be devised free from flaws. As soon as servants are accustomed to a place and discover its weak points, some of them are sure to turn these defects to their own advantage. This remark applies more particularly to public establishments than to any other. At the same time there is no large commercial house anywhere that is not preyed upon habitually by one or more larcenous confederacies among the hands it employs.

My own particular workhouse is an old one, and therefore abounding in defects. It was built before the requirements of such places were thoroughly understood. In consequence, some of its sections are too large, and others just as much too small, while a number of necessary offices are altogether wanting. Further, there are no architectural arrangements for completely isolating the various departments, and for preventing subordinate officials and their pauper deputies from prowling all over the place whenever they feel so inclined.

Certain necessary offices being wanting, so also are the officers. There are, therefore, no arrangements for supervising and checking a good many proceedings. As a matter of course, certain abuses were developed in the place immediately after its opening, and have continued to flourish ever since. Certain people connected with the place, indeed, have become so accustomed to peculation that they have come at length to look upon its exercise as very much a matter of right.

Perhaps no form of workhouse larceny is so objectionable as that which deals with the food of the inmates. The supplies are strictly in proportion to the numbers to be fed, such and such a quantity of potatoes, flour, oatmeal, meat, etc., per head being issued daily. Thus, if a subordinate officer should appropriate a certain quantity of the raw stuff, the portion of each individual would be correspondingly reduced; and if his or her pauper assistants made raids on the cooked food, the individual shares must undergo still further diminution.

Now, not a morsel more than is absolutely necessary to support life in a state of health is handed out to the cook. Theft of food, then, on anything like a large scale, must inevitably produce much suffering and injury to the majority of the inmates. In many workhouses, indeed, the latter are half starved, or a little more, just that a few may make illicit gains, while a few more gorge inordinately.

Nor is this all. When the rations are seriously reduced, the blame is invariably placed on the wrong shoulders. The master is set down as a barefaced thief, and, as likely as not, three or four of the guardians are condemned, in the minds of the paupers and their sympathizers, as his accomplices.

However, larceny in large establishments never attains the magnitude which it is capable of attaining until a master-mind takes its direction; and master-minds are just as uncommon in larceny as in any other walk of life. Wanting them, the plunderers steal in disjointed groups, and without that general understanding and co-operation indispensable to thoroughly effective action. Besides, there is always a jealousy between the groups, and even between members of the same group, which leads to espionage, trap-laying, and downright informing.

The master-mind, however, is sure to appear sooner or later among the scoundrels. Such a one is not long in. gaining the confidence of the various groups, and in convincing them of the manifest advantages attending united and systematic action. The plunder then becomes broader and more adroit, and more lucrative also to the principals. Methods are arranged for removing the goods from the house in the safest way, and for disposing of them to the best advantage with the safest customers; and the system once constructed, it is sure to continue in action, not only during the superintendence of the contriver, but long after he has disappeared.

There are countless ways of smuggling articles out of a workhouse. Here much depends on the quality of the persons engaged in the transaction. Manifestly it is much easier for a highly placed official than for a subordinate; while any subordinate, however mean, has many more facilities at his disposal than a pauper.

A very common method is by coming to an understanding with the contractors or their men. Then—this according to the defects of the workhouse system and the character of the officer superintending the departments attached—the stores are either delivered short of quality, or the full amount is deposited in the house and a portion conveyed away—often at the moment by the vehicles that brought them. No other method, indeed, can well be adopted where the plunder is bulky, unless the plunderers are absolutely reckless; and in the latter case they are sure to be observed, and exposed in very short space.

When the food is plundered on system by officials, this is the method adopted:—Different days are selected for the raids on the different sorts of food—one day for the meat, another for the flour, a third for the vegetables, a fourth for the meal, and so on.

Tuesday, let us suppose, is one of the porridge or gruel days. The paupers will receive precisely the same quantity morning and evening—say a pint and a half on each occasion. But the quality? The best answer to that question is a fair statement of what ought to happen, contrasted with what has happened. A pound of meal to a gallon of water is the regulation amount; but on the raiding-day the proportion is known to have been seventy pounds of meal to one hundred and twenty gallons of water, or fifty pounds of meal—nearly one-half—short.

The paupers complain; but of what use is that? The master admits that there is some justice in the complaint. He calls for the cook, and receives a plausible excuse which he does not care to search too closely, orders that the thing shall not occur again, and then forgets all about it. Next day the gruel is all correct, and the next, and the next, until the raiding-day returns, when what has just been described is repeated.

It is the same with the meat, which is stolen on one of the days when there is soup for dinner; and the same with everything eatable.

Of course this sort of thing cannot take place without the notice and connivance of the paupers employed in the kitchen. Of course, also, the said paupers do not fail to take full advantage of what is going on. Seeing their superiors steal the raw food, they do just the same with the cooked food. They carry it off by wholesale, gorge themselves till they can gorge no more, and sell the rest openly to such paupers as can purchase, while the impecunious have to look on, half famished, regarding the whole thing in their own perverse way.

The pilferers are envied. At the same time there is hardly one who suffers by their conduct who does not say to himself, 'If I were in the place of one of these people, I would do precisely the same thing. My turn may come some day; and it would be a folly in me were I to do aught to spoil the game by which I hope to profit as they.'

Besides the way of thinking just described, there is the common repugnance to playing the part of informer. This repugnance, by the way, the thieves take care to raise to the highest pitch, and maintain there, by discoursing upon and denouncing the odious part at every turn, and still more by denouncing and persecuting a supposed informer in every way.

There are two or three supposed informers always undergoing the tyranny of the dishonest, and the general persecution of their fellows, in every badly conducted workhouse. And in ninety-nine cases out of a hundred the poor fellows are no informers at all, but mere scapegoats on whom the real informers—themselves in all likelihood thieves jealous of rivals—have contrived to fix suspicion.

A London workhouse dining-hall.

Now and again, when the half-starved begin to grumble too loudly, the grumbling is very effectually put down by those interested, in the following ingenious way. They fix upon a few of the loudest-tongued, and soon find the means of subjecting them to all the pains and penalties awarded by pauper communities to people really guilty of the detested practice of informing.

As to complaints to higher authorities, they are seldom of any avail except to bring trouble, and plenty of it, down on the heads of the complainants. Poor Law Inspectors deputed to investigate such matters invariably demand evidence of a sort which paupers cannot give. An assertion that the gruel has been thin, or the soup not the thing, though supported by three-fourths of the paupers in the house, goes for nothing, taken alone. The pauper has no means of testing the precise thinness of the one or the other; no means of comparing the stuff he finds fault with, with food of the right sort. If, indeed, he could produce convincing proof that the raw material has been tampered with, he would secure all that he could possibly expect; but this is obviously altogether beyond his reach.

For my own part, I do not see why instruments on the principle of the hydrometer, for testing the density of soup and gruel, should not be placed in every pauper refectory, to be used by a selection of the more intelligent inmates previous to every soup and gruel meal. The testing would not occupy three minutes, and, with a duly kept record of results, would go far towards extinguishing dishonesty of this kind.

Dishonesty of another kind might be even more easily dealt with. I do not see why small pauper officials, employed to measure out soup, etc., should be allowed to give diminished quantities, for no other purpose than that they may be enabled to sell the surplus, at the end of the meal, to those who can afford to purchase.

Again, if the weighing out of raw food were conducted at all times under the supervision of a deputation of inmates, changed from time for reasons unnecessary to mention, much depredation would be prevented.

As things go, anyone complaining, no matter how just the cause, is set down as an ill-conditioned, grumbling, quarrelsome subject. Care, too, is taken to fix the character upon him by encouraging the really ill-conditioned and unscrupulous to annoy him at every turn. He resents, of course, which is exactly what is wanted; therefore he incurs all the blame of the dispute. This is duly represented in the 'proper quarter'—with the proper result, namely, that he is ever after regarded in that quarter as all that certain people represent him, and his complaints are henceforth treated with supreme contempt. Meanwhile, his life is made miserable in the house by all the ways which vindictive officers know how to employ. His tasks are made hard. He is called upon for extra work, when such is required. Finally, nothing that he does ever gives satisfaction. Many a man has been driven from the house into the bitterest destitution by such proceedings.

Paupers, of course, carry their outdoor vices into the house with them. Some of these find no scope for exercise therein, and therefore subside into a state of quiescence for the time; but, by way of compensation, others are developed in their stead, and some of the old ones are intensified. The already false and tricky become more so among us; the greedy grow greedier still; the slanderer flaunts in all his glory as an indoor pauper; and the thief appropriates everything upon which he can lay hands.

Theft is especially rife among the Ins and Outs; and they have more opportunities of displaying their dexterity than would readily be imagined. Indoor paupers gradually acquire various little things, as books, pocket-knives, writing materials, sets of chessmen, and so on. Much of this kind of property is carried constantly about the person—stuffed into the breast, or stowed away in pockets which the poor creatures construct in their clothes wherever it is possible to place them.

But pockets cannot be multiplied as wanted. Such property, therefore as cannot be crushed into them is stowed away in the beds, every one of which is more or less of a magazine.

When an In and Out is about to discharge himself, he ascertains quietly which bed contains the more valuable articles; and, let the owner watch as he will, the thief will contrive to get at his hoard and strip it of whatever has excited his cupidity.

Workhouse property suffers, too, from the depredations of these gentry. It was only the other day that one of them was arrested in the receiving ward, with a number of knives and forks on his person. The articles bore the workhouse stamp, were much worn, and would not have brought the thief more than a couple of pence, even supposing that he could find a 'fence' who would venture to purchase. Nevertheless, he stole them, and being detected, as already mentioned, was brought immediately before a magistrate and sentenced to two months' imprisonment for the paltry trick.

Workhouse knives, however, are always disappearing from their proper shelves, though they do not always find their way outside. Hungry men, and those in want of tobacco, will sell whatever they possess in order to gratify their cravings. Thus go many of the pocket-knives brought into the house.

A pocket-knife of some sort, however, is indispensable to every man here. The workhouse knives, therefore, are taken, the blades broken in half, and the portion attached to the handle ground down to a point; while a little sulphuric acid, begged or bought from the pauper superintendent of the painter's shop, enables the owner of this peculiar weapon to efface the workhouse mark from the steel.

One of the peculiarly dangerous vices of indoor paupers is their habit of shifting the blame of their own misdeeds on to the shoulders of others. They are always watching one another, and always betraying, too. This is done—sometimes in vindictiveness, sometimes in envy, and sometimes in sheer malice—for the mere sake of doing mischief to their neighbours. Tale-bearing, as already mentioned, is a common vice; and the grand object of the tale-bearers is to fix the odium of their actions on somebody else.

Curiously enough, one particular individual is spontaneously selected by all the members of the gang. Possibly three or four of them agree on ascribing the offence to him; but in most cases there is no such pre-arrangement. The individual is, as a rule, a man who will have nothing to do with the gossips, or who has won the hostility of one or other of them. This one—the person provoked—then goes whispering from man to man, 'Such and such is a tale-bearer; beware of him.' That is sufficient. The other gossips hasten to take up the cry; thus it soon becomes general.

So much done, the rascals set to work reporting one another by wholesale to the officers; and every act of this kind is set down, without fail, to the credit of the unfortunate person already indicated. Gradually the animosity of the whole of the males is excited against him. The end generally is that he is set upon, by pre-arrangement, in some convenient place, where his assailants are sure of being able to do what they have in hand without interruption. He is brutally treated, it needs hardly be told.

Afterwards the odium in which the unfortunate man has been held dies rapidly away. It is soon generally admitted that a mistake has been made, and that the man never did anything of the kind attributed to him. When matters reach this stage, the rascally talebearers look out for another scapegoat, who, when it suits them, has to undergo precisely the same treatment.

And these scoundrels are allowed to do this with perfect impunity. The officers of a workhouse, from the porter with his uniform and twenty-five pounds a year, upwards, are all of the most lordly description. Without exception, they regard all paupers as of quite an inferior order of beings—creatures much lower in the scale of creation than the pigs which fatten at their expense. They are not admitted to have rights—not even the right to cherish feelings of any sort. It never enters an officer's head that, there can be gradations of character in a workhouse. In his high and mighty view, there is no better or best among its inmates, but all stand alike on the same exceedingly low level. They are all alike repulsive—wretches who have no just claim to life, since it merely enables them to be burdensome to the ratepayers. It is their duty, considers the officer, to accept their task-work and modicum of food, and the contumely that accompanies them, with clasped hands and on bended knees.

These high-minded officers—task-masters at forty pounds a year and so on—quite forget that if there were no paupers there would be no workhouses, and not the smallest necessity for such comfortable posts as those they hold.

Paupers, I repeat, are all equal in the eyes of the officers, which is a way of regarding matters that tells admirably in favour of the scoundrels. In consequence, if the latter conceive a grudge against a person better conducted than themselves, and for no other reason than that he is better conducted, and if they gratify their grudge by slandering him first, and thus rendering him detestable to the mass of his fellow-inmates, and then—having thus prepared the ground—by assaulting him, nothing ever comes of it. In the view of the officers it is all a pauper's brawl, and nothing more, and the parties to it—the assailants and the assailed—are treated exactly alike; either all sent about their business after a sham hearing, or all subjected to the same punishment.

This when no great harm is done. Should the thing, however, end seriously—as sometimes happens—officers and culprits unite in blackening the character of the sufferer, and making him out the only one to blame.

Lying, slandering, meanness of all sorts, cowardly conspiracies and caballings, and greed are eminently pauper vices. So is skulking. No man will do his own work, if he can by any trickery pass it over to a neighbour, or shirk it altogether.

CHAPTER X.
CURIOUS PAUPERS.

THE workhouse abounds in curiosities of humanity. Conspicuous among these are the clever men, of whom there are quite a number. Within my view at this moment there are witty story-tellers, acute disputants, and showy scholars. There are men who make you wonder how they could have failed so signally in life, as it is clear they have done. Nor are these among the educated only. There are artisans possessing first-rate skill in their respective crafts; men whom, as it would appear to you— masters would be glad to employ, and few of whom are past their prime.

One remains astonished at their position as indoor paupers, for a week or so; but when you come to know them your wonderment ceases. They are all men with grievances which, as narrated by themselves, are very great grievances indeed, and tell with exceeding force against the authors. However, examine the conduct of these grievance-mongers to one another, and you will soon understand the men and the reason why they are indoor paupers.

With just a few remarkable exceptions, they are sharp—the sharpest of practitioners. The ordinary task-work is easy to them; but, on principle, they never complete it under any circumstances. Give one of them four pounds of oakum to pick, and he will get through two pounds; give him two pounds, and he will contrive to leave half undone. Again, employ them in odd jobs about the house, and they spin them out endlessly, contriving the while to put all that is really toilsome in them on others; meantime they bustle about, in appearance the busiest of men, but in reality doing next to nothing. Yet for all that they rebuke and order about their quieter and more industrious mates, when there happens to be an officer within earshot, in such an artful way that the said officer, if anything of a novice, is sure to attribute delays and scamping of work to any rather than the real culprits.

It is just the same with them when the work is over. They are eternally intent on securing the greater share of whatever good things are going. They will have the choicest seats by the fire in winter, and insist on monopolizing the coolest corners in summer. Then, in the workhouse, tobacco is the chief male want: men are continually selling their food in order to procure the means of obtaining it. The clever paupers, who are all very greedy ones, take advantage of this whenever they can, buying dinners, bread, etc., on credit—from the greenest hands, be it understood, for nobody else will trust them—and never paying the price. They will also borrow anything and everything on the same terms.

These fellows are continually squabbling among themselves about one thing or another--the dispute being invariably a case of diamond cut diamond; but they band as one against everybody else—supporting one another in chicanery, *finesse*, browbeating, and in roaring down an individual too new to the house to have comrades, and who nevertheless dares to resent being 'bested,' or, in other words, bamboozled by one of the fraternity.

There you have the sum and substance of their grievances, and the cause of their failure in life. *No master can trust them: no men of the same calling care to work with them.* They are none of them actual thieves, so far as anybody but themselves is aware. No conviction is on record against a single one. They have always been too shrewd to commit themselves: far too clever and cautious to allow themselves to be found out. But a little contact soon shows masters and men that, in dealing with these gentry, they must 'keep all their eyes open,' and their wits continually at work, as otherwise these exceedingly clever fellows are sure to be in them.'

Neither masters nor men, however, can afford to be eternally on the watch. Such a course would involve too great a waste of time and brains, and would therefore interfere very seriously with the business of the moment. The one and the other, therefore, prefer to steer clear of the clever ones. The master will not employ them when circumstances allow him a choice; and the men follow his example, either getting up a strike against the dangerous fellows, or making common cause against them to render the job a misery so far as they are concerned, and thus compel them to 'cut it.' That is why they are here: but enough of them.

Here is another curiosity of quite a different sort. He is a young man of remarkably athletic frame, with fine features and large, melancholy eyes. He is solitary in his habits, and refuses to be drawn into conversation. Yet he is noted even here for courage and resolution—a man who has few equals in a stand-up fight, and who can take any amount of punching without seeming to feel it in the least. Generally speaking, he is the quietest and most orderly of men. Now and again, however, an insubordinate devil takes possession of poor Harry, and woe to those who cross him for the time. It is easy to know when he is thus. His eyes become bloodshot, and all his motions jerky, while his features are set and his mouth drawn as though cast in iron. Perceiving these indications, the officers foresee that there is a bad time before them.

Harry lays himself out for a collision with them in all sorts of ways that are most provoking—does his task negligently, is rude when spoken to, and takes to lying about in the midst of working-hours, and precisely in the places where he is most likely to attract attention. Truculence, indeed, is manifest in every feature and every action of the man.

The officers are forbearing in the extreme, but they merely delay the outbreak. He is sure to compel one or other of them into noticing his doings, and then at the first word of reproof he flames up. There is a tussle, and a fierce one. Harry goes for the officer, who defends himself as best he can, trying the while to grapple with and hold his assailant until assistance comes, hurting him as little as he can. The pair are sure to go to the ground, where they lie rolling over and over, until others reach the scene, often to be floored likewise.

At length the madman is secured and marched off to the padded room. Here he is left in quiet for a few hours; and always with the best effect. When the officer comes to release him, he finds Harry the same calm, silent, obedient fellow as he is at all times, except when the fit is upon him. He does not even seem to remember the outbreak, but returns to his place among the other inmates as if nothing had happened.

Poor Harry! His sweetheart and himself were passengers in the ill-fated *Princess Alice* when she was run down by the *Bywell Castle*. He was saved, while she—evidently the better fated of the two—was drowned.

That, indeed, was a catastrophe. But, as waterside men are wont to remark when recalling it, 'the *Bywell Castle* never had no luck arterwards.' They changed her name, but could not alter her doom. She went down with all hands a few years later. It is a sure proof, in their estimation, that she was wholly to blame for the collision.

This brings me to another of our pauper curiosities—one who has suffered also from the collision mentioned, though in quite another way. He is a fine, powerful fellow, who, as himself often remarks, 'does not know the end of his own strength.' He is master of three or four crafts, being an accomplished lighterman among the rest, and is full of native shrewdness besides.

Having been employed ashore when the collision occurred, and close to the spot, he was called upon daily—at first almost hourly—to lend a hand in bringing ashore the bodies of the victims. This went on for weeks; and what tales he tells of his experiences! As, for instance, of bodies of women picked up with fingers cut off, not in the shock or in the terrible death-struggle that followed, but by prowlers who fished them up in the dark, secured all that was valuable about them, severing the fingers as the readiest way of possessing themselves of rings, and then flinging the carcases back to the all-devouring river.

Couples, too—ay, whole groups—occasionally came to the surface locked together in the grapple of death.

'We had to break their arms,' the man explained, 'in order to sunder them.' The while his lip quivers and his eye moistens, as various scenes connected with the dread event rise before him.

He stood it for a week or two without flinching—being at that date 'hard as nails,' as he expresses it, in mind no less than in muscle. But the long-protracted ordeal told on even him at length, breaking him down at once and completely, 'like a shot,' he says, transforming him from one of the firmest and most fearless of men into a nerveless, trembling coward, and driving him from his employment, and indeed from the waterside whereabouts it lay for the most part, from that time forth and for ever.

His heart has been as water ever since in the face of difficulties. He has lost all enterprise. He dare not encounter a risk by water. He cannot merely look the river in the face. He is in consequence, though yet under thirty, and, as already stated, probably the strongest and most active man among us, useless to himself and to everybody else—one of our confirmed Ins and Outs, in short.

A curiosity of quite another order is old Rannock, the capitalist and usurer of the house. He is tall and gaunt—'The Living Skeleton,' as he is named by way of alternative—with a long bony face and the most relentless of mouths, ay, and of hearts too. His is a countenance that does not belie him in the least.

Most of the inmates have friends who give them a shilling or two monthly when they call, and who send them postage stamps now and again; and old Rannock has made it his business, for ten or fifteen years past, to transfer as much of both to his own possession as is at all possible.

He retails tobacco, snuff, stationery, etc. It is also whispered that anyone having the means, and who can be thoroughly trusted, may even obtain a dram from this workhouse chapman. All his goods, it is scarcely necessary to remark, are the very worst of their kind. Nevertheless, they are sold by him at the dearest rate. For instance, he purchases envelopes at about threepence the hundred, and paper at eighteen-pence the ream; and he sells a single envelope and sheet of paper for a halfpenny. Thus he secures a profit of 1s. 9d. on every hundred envelopes he disposes of, and of 18s. 6d. on every ream of paper.

It is just the same with other articles, notably matches. These he will only sell loose, at a halfpenny the score; and much he grumbles when cold weather and short days, necessitating fires, and in the evening lights, interrupt this branch of his business for the winter.

As to stamps, he will purchase them from their possessors for prices varying with the wants of the latter, and he sells them again for three-halfpence to twopence each, according to the demand. He deals also in needles and thread, and especially in pocket-knives. The latter articles are essential to the comfort of indoor paupers, and old Rannock compels such as deal with him for them to pay through the nose. It is a common thing for a man in straits, for tobacco say, to sell him a knife for a trifle— from a halfpenny to threepence—the latter being the largest sum he ever gives, and buy it back again in a day or two at an advance of 500 or 1,000 per cent., according to the quality of the article.

In this way old Rannock has realized quite a fortune. It is well known that he could quit the house and live comfortably on his savings, were he so minded. He is the owner of half-a-dozen houses, and has a balance in the bank besides. He speaks of 'retiring from business' too, 'shortly' is his common expression to-day, as for several years past. But the end of the term of his indoor-pauper life never draws any nearer. He is fettered to it by his greed of gain; and no doubt will die in it.

He goes out now and then, 'for a holiday,' as he explains; but in reality to look after his property, and procure supplies of the wares in which he deals. That is all that he sees of the world without. As to relatives and friends, he is never visited by anybody, and never receives a single letter from year's end to year's end.

He has appropriated a corner, and there he sits, when delivered from task-work, doing his 'business.' It is the same on Sundays as on week-days. He never goes to church, and pays not the smallest attention to the missionaries or preachers. However, he accepts with avidity the tracts they distribute, and will even ask for more, because they serve him as wrappers for tobacco, snuff, and loose matches, etc.

Books he values merely as articles of commerce. Nobody ever saw him open one, except to ascertain its condition previous to purchasing.

So he exists, intent on adding penny to penny, and never giving a thought as to what is to come eventually of himself and his gains.

Now for our strong-minded paupers—atheists, materialists, or whatever else you may call them. We have three or four, who acknowledge as their leader one of Fergus O'Connor's original Chartists. This person is a mechanic—a little, old, hard-headed man, with a remarkably mean-looking countenance. His physiognomy struck me from the first as characteristic. He has the piggish eyes, and the short, aggressive-looking nose, peculiar to his kind. He is a shareholder in the Rickmansworth estate to the amount of £100, but is never a penny the better of it. What is more, he is never likely to be, and owns it. The estate is in the hands of a receiver, and likely to remain there. Such men as my leading atheist can never get any answer from him, except that he is 'improving the estate.'

My little acquaintance—I hardly care to call him friend—and his followers amuse themselves chiefly by framing difficult questions wherewith to bother all howlers who visit us on

Sunday evenings. And that they do bother them very considerably is beyond a doubt. The worst of the matter is, that the said howlers never will confess their inability to deal with such queries as, 'Is it possible for mind to exist independent of matter?'—one of several of the like sort put to them a short time ago—but attack them with all the confidence of the most presumptuous ignorance, and therefore fail signally in their answers.

Such presumptuous ignorance, and such egregious failure, is precisely what the freethinkers lay themselves out for; and they are only too skilful in using both as aids in unsettling the religious belief of their companions.

As to the knowledge and capacity of these gentry, they are both about as mean as possible. They have got hold of a few stock atheistic arguments, or rather of the conclusions deduced from these arguments, and mostly in a limping way; but they are sufficient for them. All the reasons you can adduce to the contrary have no effect on them. If they find that you have a good knowledge of the subject, and are able to handle it with effect, they avoid you; and that is all.

They seem, one and all, to be really anxious for utter extinction at the close of their miserable earthly existence; which, to my poor thinking, is about the meanest as well as most curious aspiration that human beings can entertain.

Now and again I cannot help asking myself why they wish to be extinguished. It is a thought which suggests others—as to the lives of these men, and how they have used their opportunities for doing good and evil. But enough of them.

There is no more curious personage in the house than our quack, if I may term him so. Perhaps empiric would be a better epithet. He is one who confirms several speculations suggested to me by the annals of the darker ages, long before I entered this house.

He is of Jewish descent, short and robust in figure, and possessing a head and face indicative of no common intellect, energy, resolution, and concentration of purpose, though with very little that is peculiarly Jewish about them. There is no superabundance of blubber anywhere, and no tallow in the complexion. The skull is dome-shaped, spreading broadly, as well as rising high. The countenance is triangular, and strikes you as a whole. You do not fix on any particular feature. It is remarkably keen, and as remarkably cautious, yet not in any way hesitating or indirect. The hair, in spite of the age—over sixty—is still red, the eyes are blue, and the cheeks ruddy. He looks, on the whole, far more like a good specimen of the Danish breed than what he is.

Nor is this man the first Jew in whom I have noticed little or nothing of the physique of his race. Indeed, it is only in countries where they keep much to themselves, because they must—because intercourse with them is a thing detestable to the people among whom they dwell—that they preserve the Hebrew physiognomy and build. In England Jewish families, especially of the lower order, are Jew in little beyond the name. How this comes to pass with a people who so seldom intermarry with native races, physiologists must explain.

My Jew indoor-pauper bears a name indicating that he comes of the highest and most exclusive Jewish caste. However, he has long ceased to belong to the community, or he would not be here. He is a freethinker, in fact, and one of the most advanced school. He has nothing in common, however, with our other freethinkers, whom he disdains and avoids. Neither does he flaunt his views in public, or seek to make converts. They appear only in the shape of terse and pointed sneers at all faiths in which he indulges at rare intervals.

Like the rest of his race, he was by profession a trader, devoting himself to the species of commerce which best suited his locality and condition—that of marine-store dealer. Had he confined himself to it, no doubt he would have realized a competence at least. But he gave much of his time and energy to certain pleasures, and much more to the profession of far-back ancestors.

He comes, indeed, of a family of Jew physicians, who were renowned twelve to fifteen centuries ago, and he is in possession of a few of their secrets, which have been transmitted from father to son down to him. He dealt in these, as in marine stores, from the day he first started in life, and soon acquired a name among his neighbours as one who could cope with a number of common complaints far more successfully than the most accomplished physicians of his vicinity.

He was particularly great in dealing with rheumatism and skin diseases, and especially in dealing with that terrible disease which punishes sexual immorality. Indeed, his practice here convinces me that the said disease is identical with the 'leprosy' of the middle ages, and therefore was not imported from America by the sailors of Columbus, as is commonly supposed.

Mr. Elias, I repeat, soon won a high repute among his neighbours as a leech; but as these neighbours were all of the humbler classes, and as the licensed members of the healing profession were never weary of denouncing him as a dangerous quack, he was shunned of the better classes until the advent of the cholera.

I have long believed that this epidemic is identical with 'the plague' of the far past, and that, though the said plague reappeared with variations at different times, and so obtained different names, it was always substantially the same. So it seems believed the Jewish physicians, who alone were capable of ministering with success to those whom it attacked.

When it devastated the east of London some twenty years ago, Mr. Elias at once came forward to wrestle with it after the manner of his ancestors, and with astonishing success. He boasts that not a single patient treated by him died; and there are thousands ready to bear witness that the boast is a fact. Even his rivals, the regular practitioners of the quarter, were obliged to admit it.

Public attention was drawn to the matter, and an investigation into his merits followed. In result, he was recognised by the profession as competent to deal with a limited number of diseases, and his name was admitted to the Medical Directory.

He was now on the high road to fame and fortune, when-- But it is no part of my purpose to tell how and why he failed to use his great opportunities. All I shall state is that he is now totally forgotten, in broken health, and subject to fits—in all respects about the most helpless of our indoor paupers. He has no friends, and his relatives have abandoned him.

Still his intellect is strong; he is master of his medical secrets, and, as several recent cases show, of the skill to use them properly. He might still secure a comfortable position, did he choose to sell these secrets; but he is as careful of them as ever, resolute that they shall die with him. To this end he has always insisted on compounding and administering his drugs himself. He will not even trust the empty cup into another hand until he has cleansed it thoroughly. He will give nobody the smallest chance of carrying away a drop for analysis.

For the last twelve or eighteen months his attention has been strongly attracted to the ravages of cholera in Southern Europe, and he has made many efforts to bring his special qualifications under the notice of various governments; but as he cannot himself hold a pen, and is obliged to employ a brother-pauper, who in nine cases out of ten is quite illiterate, it is not to be wondered at that, considering the quality of the letters, and the place whence they emanate, they should never draw a single reply.

So my old Hebrew, who has ceased to be a Jew, and who is in possession of such invaluable secrets, remains, and is likely to remain for the rest of his life, an utterly useless indoor pauper, unless, indeed, the reappearance of cholera in England should cause a demand for him, and so restore him to notoriety.

Impostors? We have plenty, and of all sorts. Here are mathematicians incapable of distinguishing between a sine and a tangent; Latinists who cannot construe the first line of Virgil's great poem; heroes who never carried steel; and officers to whom the elements of drill and tactics are complete mysteries. There is nothing easier than to detect the falseness of the pretences of these fellows: a few quiet questions will always do that. Yet they pass for what they announce themselves with masses here, who, in consequence, hold them in great respect; and the rascals themselves are satisfied.

Not ten minutes ago I heard one of them astonishing a group of ten or twelve with a discourse upon things in general, compounded of the axioms of Euclid, mottoes of great houses taken from the Peerage book, and three or four quotations from Bacon's Essays—the last not given as quotations, however, but as the genuine productions of the speaker's brain. It would have been worse than useless interfering here and exposing the knave. Not having a copy of the Essays at hand in support of the assertion that he was quoting, he would have been certain to meet it with a point blank and offensive denial, clenched with a string of oaths; and, as I happen to know from experience, the denial and the execrations would have carried it against me with the mob. He was typical here.

Even were it not so, I do not think there would have been any good in contradicting the man. Axioms, mottoes, and quotations of that sort are not likely to do much mischief, nor is the object they are intended to further one to provoke much hostility. Such knaves merely want to swagger a little; and if there be a good deal of white lying used in raising one's self to the swaggering-point, what does that matter? It pleases the fellow, and does not hurt me.

Impostors of a more reprehensible order, however, abound. I could lay my hands on half-a-dozen thorough rogues, who possess property sufficient to support themselves decently outside, yet who thrust themselves in here for no other purpose than just to add to their wealth.

Here is one old fellow who, up to a few months ago, contrived to make a couple of widows maintain him in comfort. They kept a sweet-shop between the three, the two women taking it in turn to look after the shop, while one of them—the one off duty—was about town enjoying herself with the gay old fellow. So things went on for years, until one of the widows died suddenly. Then the other, appalled by the catastrophe, thought it time to look after her soul, and the partnership was dissolved. The surviving widow retired to friends in the country, having the wherewithal to live at her ease for the rest of her life; and the old fellow incontinently took refuge in the workhouse, where he nurses his annuity—a very comfortable one—for the present, and whence he makes frequent excursions in search of a second couple of widows with means to consort with him on the same terms as the former couple. A shrewd old scamp, that!

Here is another capitalist of a different kind. He is a man between forty and fifty, with a long, straight, and very thin nose and a thoroughly effeminate expression of countenance. He is womanly all over, in fact, with the exception that he carries a plentiful crop of whiskers; voice mild, soft and low; figure buxom as that of a well-kept matron of the same age; manners silky, tread precisely that of a demure maiden who has overpassed her prime without entering, as yet, into the period of 'the sere and yellow leaf.' This personage is godly withal, and temperate in the extreme.

He is unmarried, for three reasons. In the first place, he never felt that way inclined; in the second place, he was always far too Miss Mollyish for a girl of spirit to take him in hand and marry him in spite of himself (a thing which girls of spirit often do with men of a certain stamp); but, chiefly, he had an ancient female relative of the right-shrewish order to keep a tight hold of him, and to warn off everybody, especially those of her own sex, who seemed at all likely to obtain an influence over him.

Always steady, hard-working, self-denying, and thoroughly trustworthy, therefore always in good employment, and eternally adding shilling to shilling, the man—if man he be—gradually acquired goods and chattels. His passion was freehold property, and one after another he laid tight hold of plot after plot of right good sort, and almost on his own terms.

Meanwhile, he opened a shop, and handed over the management to the ancient shrew; and directly she obtained the handling of money over the counter, this lady, who was no less precise and pious than the man himself; astonished all her neighbours by developing an inordinate liking for the gin-bottle.

Her drinking played the deuce with the shop. But nothing else suffered. The man retained his employment and his accumulations still. Even his losses, so far as the shop was concerned, did not amount to much. Nevertheless, they so preyed upon his mind as to reduce him to a pitiable state of melancholy. In the end, one or two friends thought the best thing they could do with him was to place him for a time, at least, in a pauper-lunatic asylum.

They took this course, thinking that his property was limited to a single house, the rent of which was certainly not sufficient to support him.

A few months in the lunatic asylum did him a world of good, and thence he was relegated to the workhouse, in order that his cure might be completed. Here he was an object of much interest to the authorities, on account of his high character and his troubles,' and some little, too, on account of his small' property.

Bit by bit, however, and much to the astonishment of everybody—and I incline to think of the man himself, no less than other people—the 'small' property turned out to be not so very small after all. One day a gentleman made his appearance in the house, to hand him over a handsome sum, as the ground-rent of certain building sites, of which nobody had ever heard before. Another day, a second gentleman applied for an interview with him, on an exactly similar errand. And so matters went, until it turned out that the half-demented, nerveless indoor pauper possessed a very nice income, instead of a paltry £15 or £20, as was at first supposed. This, too, not for a term, but, as the law hath it, for ever. Nor, as it is strongly suspected, have the friends of this very poor fellow yet arrived at the end of their discoveries in this direction.

Still, this man is not at all blamed by reasonable people. I myself consider him no more than an involuntary impostor. I do not believe that he ever suspected for a moment how much was the aggregate sum of his accumulations; I verily believe, too, that during the period of his dementation many of his business transactions slipped completely out of his mind. As it happened, they were all of the soundest description, founded without exception on the most solid basis, totally free from the smallest element of speculation, and therefore certain —as it has proved—to flow to their author without any seeking on his part.

But there are so many curiosities around me that I should never have done, were I to go through them all. I have merely glanced at the most striking and typical cases. And with one more of them I shall conclude a chapter that has expanded to dimensions far larger than I intended for it at the outset.

My pensioner, Mac—, is exactly fifty years of age, and was born in a remote quarter of Argyleshire. He stands five feet eleven, and possesses an admirably proportioned figure, with a face to match. He must have been a model of manly beauty in his prime; and, in spite of his years and troubles, remains a very handsome fellow. Notwithstanding his grizzled locks, his features have not lost their youthful look; his form retains most of its grace, and it was eminently graceful; and his step is still elastic.

He is clever withal—very clever; the nearest approach to a genius, without actually being that strange thing, that I ever encountered. He was trained as a lithographer, and is a perfect master of his craft. This means much—as that he is master of drawing, free hand and mechanical, and an adept in mixing colours and laying them on—very much of an artist, in fact. He can string together, by the yard, very tolerable rhymes. He abounds in quaint humour, is terse and epigrammatic in expression, and, considering his experiences, is singularly free from coarseness of idea or speech. Intensely Scotch, he abounds in stories of the old, old time, and can sing in rare style all the finer old Jacobite lyrics. This is much, but it is not all.

He entered the Royal Engineers when he was eighteen, and served his full time—twenty-one years—spending a considerable period attached to Sandhurst College. In consequence of this service, he is dexterous in many crafts. He is a bit of an architect, a bit of a bricklayer, a bit of a blacksmith, and a bit of a carpenter—a good bit in each instance. Besides, he can knot and splice as well as an experienced seaman, has been accustomed all through his service to make the most of his materials, and to supply by various cunning devices whatever may be lacking. He is full of shift and contrivance, indeed, in everything save the business of life, where he remains as straightforward and simple as a child.

Good in many things, he is far and away best as house-painter, being particularly strong in graining and lettering. Withal, he is good-tempered and obliging, and, like all men of his peculiar temperament, active and industrious—one who cannot be idle for the life of him. In short, he is just the man that—as the saying goes—a master would jump at with avidity.

He has his failings, of course, or rather had them—his liking for good fellowship being the chief. It is an old soldier's fault, however, and his experience here has done much to cure him of it. For the rest, he is open-hearted, generous without stint to men of the like mould, and true as steel to a comrade.

And how, it will be asked, did such a man contrive to get into the workhouse?

The tale is but too readily told. However, before sketching it I must remark that here he is fast—one of the few unwilling indoor paupers that I have encountered. Though absolutely detesting the place, he cannot get out of it, try as he may. And he has tried, and is still trying with might and main, though, by this, well-nigh hopelessly.

Being the man that I describe, a prime favourite with his officers, and yet in his prime—yet under forty—when he quitted the service he had no difficulty in obtaining a comfortable appointment. In this he did very well for a time. However, his wife and a most promising son were cut off within a few months of each other; and he, poor man, fierce and reckless as a mountaineer, in his grief betook him without restraint to the bottle.

He lost his health and his appointment together, was laid on his back by a disease of the nerves, which for a period deprived him of sight and of the use of his feet, and remained prostrate for many months.

In this position, finding himself at length without a shilling or a friend to whom he could trust himself, he became—partly as a matter of prudence and partly as a matter of necessity —an inmate of this house. Here he was carefully looked to and nursed back into health.

Once upon his legs, he found himself in good hands. The master—himself an old soldier—sympathised heartily with him; and the guardians, as a matter of course, beheld him through the eyes of the master. Now that he was convalescent, he was bound to do something, and, as the lightest task that could be assigned, he was appointed to look after the painting of the building—a work always in progress. Here he gave complete satisfaction; and the guardians, at the suggestion of the master, allowed him to draw the whole of his pension.

It was expected that he would employ the money in regaining his independence; but Mac did nothing of the kind. He took his discharge, and went out—to take to the bottle the moment he was across the threshold, and to stick to it while he had a penny left. A sad thing, but inevitable, all things considered. The man was still very shaky—and in brain no less than body; and his grief, exasperated by other griefs, was still strong upon him. In short, it was hardly to be expected that, under the circumstances, he would use his money and his liberty aright.

Money spent, he became an indoor pauper once again, was received with some kindly rebuke, and restored to his old occupation. Then things went on as if nothing had occurred to spoil them. Quarter-day came, and Mac received his pension once again, and repeated his previous performance precisely. In again, he was treated as before. So, no doubt, things would have gone on—Mac doing his share of the housework, and doing it well until quarter-day came; then hey for another fortnight's spell at liberty and spreeing.

Unfortunately—or perhaps all things considered fortunately —for him, the firebrand to whom I devote a chapter, as unquestionably deserving of it, now became an inmate of the house, insinuated himself into Mac's good graces, and, as in many another case, filled his head with the most extravagant ideas respecting the rights of paupers. Among these was, that not only ought he to receive his pension in full as a matter of justice, but be paid a fair wage—say two guineas a week—for his work into the bargain. The firebrand, in fact, succeeded in persuading the poor man that the guardians were far exceeding their powers in employing him regularly as a painter, while giving him merely the allowance of a pauper —that, in short, after deducting the expense of his board and lodging, etc., they were clearing quite £1 14s. 6d. a week out of his labour, which, the scoundrel added, was no doubt charged to the Union, while somebody pocketed the cash. No wonder that, with such an adviser at his ear, the pensioner, who as yet had not recovered full strength of intellect, should become discontented.

Mac, indeed, listened eagerly to the pettifogger, believed every word he said, and, worse still, followed his advice. Thus he separated himself entirely from the friendly master, and actually sent in a bill to the guardians, amounting to many pounds, as wages for work done. It need hardly be said that the bill was received with just indignation; but that was far from being the worst part of the affair.

From that time forth, hostilities began between Mac and the authorities of the house. Following the malicious advice of the pettifogger, he petitioned every possible board for aid against them, but always in vain. Meanwhile the guardians, on their side, asserted their legal rights, and attached his pension. Ay, and they have stuck to it ever since.

Mac, now fully recovered, is supremely miserable. He sees and regrets his manifold follies. He has forsworn the bottle, and thrown aside his discontent. But the guardians, attacked as they have been by the pettifogger himself, as told in another place, and by sundry others acting under the advice of that personage, are not to be appeased. Moreover, the War Office supports them against my poor pensioner.

Mac has now no doubt, and neither have I, that were he but able to support himself out of the house for a few weeks, he would be able to secure permanent employment. But this course he cannot adopt without a little money in his pocket—a quarter's pension, say; and this much he cannot obtain.

In his despair he has applied to have his annuity commuted, according to the rules applicable to such cases. Were this done, it is his purpose to sail at once for New Zealand, where he has a brother comfortably settled, and where a man of his varied and highly practical attainments could hardly fail to prosper. In reply, the War Office authorities tell him that they are prepared to grant his request, so soon as he can prove to their satisfaction that he can support himself out of doors by his own exertions, which, as he very justly objects, is precisely what he cannot do, so long as his pension is withheld from him.

Mac 'cannot get out;' in short, so far as he can see, he is condemned to indoor pauperism for the rest of his life. True, he has brought all his woes on himself. Still, his case is a hard one, and deserving of commiseration. Is there nobody of influence to help him?

Chapter XI.
A Thorough Vagabond.

Besides our permanent inmates and our Ins and Outs, we have also a sprinkling of 'occasionals.' These are people who spend much of their time in wandering the country over, and who make themselves indoor paupers during the harsher winter months, when cadging is out of the question; and now and again in summer, when their garments, or the more essential portions thereof—as shoes, etc.--require renewal.

By far the most remarkable of our occasionals is Stumpy Bluff. He was born a vagabond, was endowed by nature with a positive passion for scamping and roving, and with all the qualities necessary for getting through his enterprises comfortably.

Belonging to the lower middle class, he was respectably brought up, and carefully educated to fill the position of millwright—a profession which in his youth was as good as most, but which has since been merged to a great extent in that of the engineer.

Quick and clever, he mastered all the details of the trade in short space; but there was no getting him to stick to it steadily. Even during his apprenticeship he absconded to play Bamfylde Moore Carew in all directions, but invariably returned to the shop when the fit was over. 'Out of his time,' he gave full swing to his darling propensity for five years or more. At length, when about twenty-six, he took it into his head to marry during a visit to his native town; and his friends fondly hoped that he would now settle down and prosper, as he was eminently fitted to do. All in vain. Thereafter he became, if possible, more of a vagabond than ever.

And now a word or two as to his special fitness for the career that he preferred. He could sing an infinity of good songs, and tell endless good stories; he could fiddle and dance; he was an

111

adept in juggling tricks, and in managing puppets; he was a bit of a ventriloquist, and not a little of an actor; he was 'first rate' at fisticuffs, and much of a horse-chaunter; he was full of resource and readiness; above all, he was possessed of boundless impudence—or, as he prefers to call it, 'cheek.' Finally, though not exactly what you would call a dishonest man or an audacious reprobate, he was given to gratifying his various appetites to the full whenever an opportunity offered, without allowing scruples—or indeed any consideration save the always paramount one of personal safety—to restrain him.

Expert as he was in numerous avocations, Billy Bluff—he was not yet Stumpy—never found any difficulty in obtaining employment, whenever it pleased him to return to his wife and settle down for a while, which he did regularly during the winter months.

Mrs. Bluff, it may be as well to explain, kept a small-ware shop, and thus supported herself and her children decently. She never failed to welcome the vagabond on his return, as a good wife should; and never inquired too curiously into his adventures while on the road.' On his side, he was sure to return in good case, with a tolerable suit on his back, and a fair sum of money in his pocket. His pack also was well stored, especially with little presents for herself and the youngsters; and with these she made herself contented, like the prudent woman that she was.

During the cold weather, the vagabond was a model husband and father, and a model citizen too. He worked hard in his employment, attended church regularly, saw that the children went to school, and out of doors discharged all the public duties that fell to him with zeal and success. Indeed, considering his 'gift of the gab,' his natural talents, his manifold experiences, his restless activity, and his capacity for assimilating the sentiments of those around him, as also his geniality and his power of swaying most of those with whom he came in contact, there is no doubt but that he would have risen to the foremost place among his fellow-townsmen, could he only have brought himself to adhere steadily to his occupation.

However, as soon as the spring began to open, the sunshine to smile, and the blossoms to appear, Billy Bluff felt the spirit of adventure rising within him, and urging him forth with an impulse that he could not resist. Off he went, then, early in the morning of some fine Monday, hardly bidding 'good-bye' to his family, and never saying a single word respecting his destination or the route he intended to take.

A typical 'Gentleman of the Road'.

And hardly would the news of the vagabond's departure be spread through the town, ere another piece of news would be spread also, namely, that some pretty woman—mostly a young wife—had vanished much about the same time.

There were never any grounds for connecting the two flights. No previous gossip had whispered of intimacy between Billy and the runaway beauty—the pair had never been noticed in communication—never detected in secret assignations, never observed to use more than common civility—if even so much as that—towards one another.

Still everybody agreed that Billy had inviegled the woman away. There were no dissentients: it was a general impression; though whence it originated, and how it came to be general, were matters which nobody could explain.

Now and again chase was made after the female, but always ineffectually. After a mile or two all trace of her was sure to disappear, and the pursuers would return without her, as not knowing what other course to pursue.

Evidently Billy was a skilful hand at secret courtship, and as skilful also at putting everybody interested in the flight of his frail companions on the wrong scent.

As to the ultimate fate of the women, Billy would be sure to tire of each of them in a fortnight or so, abandoning her directly, without caring how, where, or what was to become of her. This generally happened some hundreds of miles from the home she had given up. Sometimes Master Bill would leave her asleep and take himself off quietly. Sometimes he would persuade her to take herself off with a tramp-acquaintance who turned up opportunely and happened to be in want of such a companion. And sometimes the rascal would beat the woman soundly, when there was no other way of getting rid of her.

As a rule the discarded paramour went headlong to the dogs, wandering anywhere and everywhere save in the direction of the friends of her virtuous days.

Delivered of the impedimenta with which he started, Billy Bluff would be in his glory. Able to turn his hand to most things rural or mechanical, he would take service for short spells—now

114

with a farmer, now with a builder, and now with a blacksmith or wheelwright--his choice being determined, for the most part, by the contiguity of the workshop to the possessor of a pleasing face and a buxom figure.

Here he would constitute himself the life and soul of the locality, and make havoc of the domestic peace of half-a-dozen households. Then, when he had made a score or more deadly enemies by intrigues conducted for the most part al fresco—for, as Billy used to remark, he delighted as much in rousing the jealousy of the chawbacons as in winning the favour of their women,—when he had effected this, I repeat, he would make a moonlight flitting in company with a favourite quean, whose connection with him was never suspected in the least, until her flight disclosed the ugly fact. I need hardly state that he would get rid of her, as of her predecessors, in a very few days.

In the course of his wanderings, Billy became a past-master in the art of illicit distillation, and as such found himself in great request wherever it pleased him to pause for a few weeks. In such a case he would secure a suitable den; or rather his clients--a confederacy of publicans doing business there-away would secure it for him—in the shape of a secluded cottage with a plentiful supply of water handy.

There would be no difficulty in procuring the plant and arranging it in working order, since he himself could do all the building-fitting and brazing required. Then, smuggling in as many casks of molasses as he required, Billy would set to work, and, in a fortnight or so, supply his patrons with as much spirits as they could dispose of in half a year. For the result of his workmanship might be passed off as brandy, whisky, rum, or gin, according to the treatment to which it was subjected after passing through the still.

Spirit-distillation over, Billy would take his fling for another fortnight or three weeks among the women of the neighbourhood, and with all the more zest and success, as being plentifully supplied with money, which, in cases without number, becomes the sinews of love as well as of war. This would continue until the feuds, in which his wooing would be sure to involve him, compelled him to show the neighbourhood a clean pair of heels.

So things went on until Billy met with the first great misfortune of his life. Up in Lancashire his attentions to some of its fascinating witches got him into trouble with a number of husbands and brothers, all of whom were colliers. The result was that three or four of the women were whacked by their irate husbands within an inch of their lives. As for Bluff, whose motto in such cases was always 'discretion,' being intercepted in his flight from the dangerous district, he was compelled, much against his will, to act as principal in what Lancashire men term an up-and-down fight.'

Now an up-and-down fight is emphatically a rough-and-tumble affair. The combatants are at full liberty to injure one another in every way. They may pull hair, scratch, bite, and, above all, kick as well as punch; and they may continue the fight on the ground, when they fall. In these affairs, the chief part is played by the feet, and as these are usually shod with clogs, or boots with heavy wooden soles, which last again are clamped with iron, terrible injuries are often inflicted in these up-and-down fights.

In this particular event Billy Bluff came off second best. His face still bears the scars of the encounter, though it took place seventeen years ago. Worst of all, one of his legs was broken to smithereens by the application of his opponent's clogs.

Our vagabond was laid up in consequence of his wounds for over a year. His damaged limb underwent amputation no less than three times—twice below the knee and once above it. During the whole of this time no tidings of him reached his native place.

He recovered at last, and hastened homewards, where his appearance, one November day—the second since he last left home—astonished all his old acquaintances, most of whom verily believed him dead, and none of whom ever expected to meet him like this, battered and broken, minus a leg, and hobbling along on crutches, and with a wooden supporter—whence his nickname, Stumpy.

Everybody, I repeat, was astonished, and Bluff himself was soon to be as much astonished as everybody else. For his wife—poor woman—concluding, like other people, that he was certainly among the gone, had married a well-to-do widower and migrated with him and her family to London.

Stumpy lost no time in following, and soon fished the party out in one of the metropolitan suburbs, where her little shop was in full swing, doing an excellent business. The children were well cared for; the wife in right good case behind her counter; while the ancient widower, smoking-cap on head and meerschaum in mouth, was taking his ease in the parlour at the back of the shop.

What passed between the three can only be surmised. An amicable arrangement, however, was speedily arrived at. The only change in the household was that room was made for the new-comer for so long as it might please him to remain. This was for the usual period, but not a moment longer.

When the ensuing spring fairly opened Stumpy was off on his travels, as of old, but not exactly in the same style. Formerly he depended for subsistence and success in favourite pursuits on his personal strength and activity. Now, however, as none knew better than he, his activity was a thing of the past, while his effective strength had diminished by at least one-half. The loss of his limb, too, had rendered him useless, or the next thing to it, in several trades. With it also had departed much of his power in amusing rude companies, and, what he valued far more, fascinating women.

But he was bound to obey his destiny and continue a vagabond; and as he did not choose to become wholly a moucher, though he had few equals and no superiors in that particular line, he determined to become a professional hawker.

The necessary license was soon procured, as also his stock-in-trade. The latter consisted of needles, thimbles, knives, scissors, and razors—all of the very worst kind. His former experiences had taught him where to procure such things at the cheapest rate, and how to sell them to the best advantage. Thus he could obtain a thousand needles for sixpence; and he could sell them again at eight a halfpenny and twenty a penny, clearing five hundred per cent at the very least on that part of his venture. Knives, razors, and scissors did not pay quite so well, though still bringing an excellent profit.

Hawking, however, was not so much a pursuit in itself as a means of pushing other pursuits, especially such as required to be covered from the view of the police. A judicious display of his wares, for instance, enabled him to make his way into quarters otherwise inaccessible. Thus he got into the kitchen of parson and squire, and very often into the parlour, too; and, in the one place as the other, Master Stumpy knew how to make the very best of his opportunity; for he was a fellow of infinite tact, with the most plausible manner in the world, and with an account of himself always ready to suit the taste of the persons with whom he happened to be in contact for the moment.

Not that Bill would condescend to play the goody-goody to anybody alive. He never affected to conceal the fact that he was a thorough scamp. On the contrary, he always let as much be understood from the very first; not vauntingly, however, but still in a comic, laughing way that won the sympathies of the listeners, whether they would or no.

As to the loss of his limb, he never, by any chance, told the truth, or even an approach to it, about that, but had twenty different stories there-anent ready to cram into the ears of his audience, each set getting the one best calculated to win its favour for the speaker.

Here it may be as well to observe that Billy was honest after a fashion. He never stuck at trifles, indeed, or neglected a safe opportunity of appropriating larger articles; but as to mere vulgar stealing, a trick that would place him in the hands of the police, or even cast a slur on his character, such an art was not to be thought of by him.

His inclination for the sex continued unabated, and he hit on a means of gratifying it without incurring any of the perils to which it used to expose him in days gone by. He had to aim much lower, however—to forego the more attractive and respectable, and the more youthful also.

Whenever he wanted to secure a female companion for a week or two while on his travels, he resorted to a plan quite common with tramps of both sexes in the like situation. This plan consisted in making his way to the nearest casual ward, and loitering about the door for half an hour or so previous to the time for opening in the evening. He seldom saw a female here exactly to his liking; but he was not too fastidious. Having made his choice, he would draw the woman into conversation, give a plausible account of himself, and obtain the outlines of her story in return: for no people in the world are more communicative than casuals among themselves; as a rule, they tell everything, without the smallest reserve, to whoever will listen.

Ten minutes' chat of this kind would be sure to display all the weak points of the poor creature to the astute Stumpy; and, acquainted with these, his fertile brain never failed to supply him with arguments strong enough to seduce her into consorting with him.

The last, it may be observed, was never any difficult task. Women given to haunting casual wards are, without exception, the most shiftless and stupid of their sex; for there are a hundred methods of avoiding these places open to women which are denied to men. Only sleepy slatterns ever get into them; and the sleepy slattern, when friendless and homeless, is about the most easily led animal in existence.

A few honeyed words in the ear, the display of a few silver coins, and a glowing account of a pleasant evening, winding up with a nice little supper, were always temptations resistless to such a woman. In short, she never failed to accept Stumpy's invitation to share them.

The supper, of course, would be preceded by a few glasses and followed by a good many; and between the eating and the drinking a bargain would be struck to the liking of both parties. Stumpy, it need not be observed, would adhere to it just so long as it suited him, and no longer, casting off his paramour in the old style whenever he felt inclined to ply 'a loose leg,' as he was wont to term rambling companions.

I have heard the rascal boast, and evidently with truth, of having formed no less than eight such connections between the beginning of April and the end of August of a single year.

From consorting with the frequenters of casual wards to becoming a frequenter himself was but an easy step, and soon made; and, growing accustomed to such places, he became careless of his business of a hawker, less of a juggler, too, and amusement manufacturer, and more and more of a moucher, until at length mouching remained his chief, almost exclusive, avocation.

But what chiefly tended to degrade Stumpy Bluff was an incident that occurred half-a-dozen years or so after the loss of his leg. On returning, as usual, from one of his rambles, towards the middle of October, he was astonished to find that the small-ware shop had changed hands, and that wife, children, and widower had taken themselves off to another hemisphere, but whether to the east or the west nobody could inform him. They were far beyond his reach, completely out of his knowledge, indeed, and so they have remained up to this very hour.

This was a sad blow to Stumpy, who, as usual of late years, had returned penniless, and very much of a scarecrow into the bargain. No alternative, indeed, was left him but to take refuge in the neighbouring workhouse for the winter. Here he played the hypocrite with such success as to win the favour of master and chaplain, and, backed by their recommendation, his petition to the board for a suit of clothing and a stock of wares to enable him to resume his hawking was granted.

Off he went once more in the spring to wander as far north as Scotland. He made his way back to the house as winter opened, and very much in the same condition as when he entered it on the first occasion. This time he did not play the hypocrite, knowing the trick to be useless. However, he had been prudent enough to retain sufficient cash to start him afresh so soon as the frost and snow should pass away.

And this kind of life he has continued to pursue ever since: in summer, a vagabond, making a circuit of hundreds of miles; in winter, an indoor pauper.

In the house, Stumpy Bluff is the life and soul of the place. There is scarcely a town in Britain south of the Forth and the Clyde which he has not visited at one time or another; nor one of which he has not amusing experiences to relate. He knows all about the charities everywhere, especially how to get at them; but he prefers chiefly to dwell on his adventures with the police and with the keepers of casual wards, both of whom he delights to chouse. He has slept in more than three hundred vagrant wards, according to his own account, and in almost as many police stations. He has 'done time,' too, generally from seven days to a fortnight; but, as he delights to observe, nobody ever succeeded in getting that detested thing, 'hard labour,' out of him. What is more, neither casual-ward master, nor policeman, nor magistrate could ever find it in his heart to be duly severe with such a remarkably comical vagabond as this one showed himself under all circumstances. More than once, as he tells with unction, all three have repented even of the small severity they were compelled to show, and to such an extent as actually to help the rascal on his way with money and garments.

But Billy, though so entertaining, is far from being edifying; very much the reverse. His ribaldry seems to increase with his years, and he is now verging on sixty. His humorous stories have sent many, not a few of them being of mature years, out of the workhouse and on to 'the road,' in the expectation of enjoying there all the loose pleasures concerning which their mentor loves to dilate. Nor are the individuals whom he has lured to such a life all males: it is notorious that he never quits the house for a ramble of any length without carrying along with him at least one of the female inmates.

Thus Stumpy Bluff has been going on for the last ten or twelve years, ever since the disappearance of his family, indeed; and thus he means to continue so long as the strength to 'keep it up' is left to him.

And then?

Who can answer that question? Stumpy himself has his own views there-anent. I can safely assert that they are not pleasant ones—gloomy in the extreme, indeed, as his remarks disclose, in spite of him, at odd times. If he does not lie down under a thicket of gorse on an out-of-the-way common, and there breathe his last, death, in all probability, will visit him in one of those infirmaries belonging to country workhouses, which, one and all, are the places that he most detests on earth. In any case, no friendly voice will ring in his dying ear, and no friendly hand close his eyes for ever. His reckless career has left him utterly alone on earth, while he dares not give a thought to heaven.

Chapter XII.
The Firebrand Pauper.

Scene, the street in front of the workhouse, and some fifty yards off; time, about two in the afternoon; dramatis person-e, one of the relieving-officers and a crowd of howling females in slovenly attire, most with bare heads. The relieving officer hurries along in front, turning his head from side to side, and ducking it now and again as an unsavoury missile flies at it. The while he yells at the top of his voice-

' Police! Police! Police!'

Somewhat in advance of the general crowd, and close at the heels of the relieving officer, scurry a pair of stalwart termagants who bear him a grudge: the one because, being in his district, she has been awarded a smaller amount of outdoor relief on her last application than on many former occasions; the other, because she has been refused relief altogether.

These two are ceaseless in their imprecations, and in volleys of the vegetable refuse with which their aprons are laden.

The crowd behind applaud with clapping hands—that is, when not engaged in supplementing the missiles of the leading harridans with others of their own.

Such scenes are common in low-lived districts. There the parochial officers generally are regarded as the natural enemies of the very poor, and the relieving officer as the chiefest enemy of all. Outside the house these gentry arc for ever liable to be assailed as described; while inside, as well as out, it is the constant study of the pauper to overreach and insult them whenever he thinks the trick may be attempted with impunity.

In fact, the rights of paupers, the best methods of asserting them, and their constant infringement by tyrant officials—all officials, without exception, being arrant tyrants in the view of paupers—are the favourite topics with this class. The information of the Indoors' on these points is absolutely astonishing in its reach and minuteness; so is their acuteness in

123

detecting wrongs ; and so also is their ingenuity in bringing derelictions of duty home to the officials who perpetrate them.

Indeed, the parish official whose duty it is to deal directly with paupers has no pleasant life of it. He has to keep his eyes open and his wits at work at every turn. He must be eternally on the watch against oversight on his own part, and against attempts to dupe him on the part of the paupers. Yet all will not avail him: he is continually falling a victim to oversight and deception. In the latter case, the pauper exults over him openly; in the former, he ought to be thankful if his enemy be satisfied with merely browbeating and bullying him in front of a crowd of other paupers. But in such a case he takes the rebuke, if he be a wise man, with becoming humility. He is well aware that, if he resent it, he is sure to have the Local Government Board appealed to, and an inquiry brought upon his shoulders, besides, in all likelihood, giving himself over to the editors of the local journals, at least, as an excellent subject for diatribe.

Indoor paupers entertain the most extraordinary ideas concerning their 'rights' and their powers of asserting them; and they are daring to the last degree in asserting these powers. Now and again one of them will go beyond all bounds in this direction, and come to grief accordingly. But he rather rejoices than otherwise in the occurrence. Henceforward he is a hero and a martyr in the eyes of his fellows. Moreover, an investigation by a superior authority, be its termination what it may, is always held by the pauper to involve a certain amount of censure on the officials whose conduct has been called in question. 'Government people would not interfere,' he reasons, 'unless they thought that there was something in it.' And then, when paupers show themselves prone to complain to superior authorities, officers will naturally become cautious in provoking such complaints, and therefore more disposed to grant the paupers' desires. Officers, indeed, however conscious of rectitude, do not like to be for ever investigated in their actions by people from outside and above; and the general result is, that the rascals given to complaining are let very much alone.

Grumbling, complaint, insult, evasion of task, advantage taken of every opportunity of inserting 'one's knife' in the flesh of an obnoxious officer—in other words, doing him as much mischief as possible—advantage also taken of every opportunity of raiding on the stores, these are things of constant occurrence in every workhouse. In different degrees, however. It is only where the establishment happens to shelter one or two specimens of what may be termed the Firebrand species of pauper that such vices attain their full proportions.

These firebrands are fellows abounding in chicanery and impudence, who are determined to live as comfortably as they can at the cost of the ratepayers, and equally determined to do as little task work and give the officers as much trouble and annoyance as circumstances will allow. Such fellows are always plausible and persuasive. They soon gain over the majority of their comrades, and by their means overawe the rest; and they invariably succeed, ere long, in reducing the whole house to a state of covert insurrection.

Perhaps as choice a specimen of the tribe as ever existed was the late Mr. Obadiah Coppersmut, an ex-solicitor's clerk, who was reduced, once upon a time, and solely by his own irrepressible cleverness in treading crooked paths, to the condition of an indoor pauper.

The house in which this genius condescended to take shelter was directed by a set of good-natured guardians, and managed by a kindly and remarkably easy-going master. The building was an old one, constructed long before the requirements of such places were thoroughly understood, and abounded, therefore, in imperfections. It was especially lacking in devices for keeping the several classes of paupers strictly to their respective quarters, and from making furtive excursions to others in which they had no business to be seen, including, in the case of some of them, the adjacent taverns.

Thanks to the errors of the constructors, it would have been impossible for the strictest of masters to maintain discipline at its proper standard; but under an easy-going régime abuses, as a matter of course, became the rule, and in these abuses a number of subordinate officials could hardly avoid being involved.

I have already remarked on the facility with which low-lived people detect the weak points of any establishment with which they may happen to be connected, and on the quickness with which they turn such defects to their own profit. I have also remarked that the depredations resulting never attain their full proportions until an organizing mind appears among the depredators. And in this instance Mr. Obadiah Coppersmut was the man; nor could anybody have been better fitted for the work.

An ex-solicitor's clerk, as already stated, he was a born pettifogger; full of contrivance and trickery; cunning as the Old Serpent, and as destitute of scruple. He was aggressive, too, and greedy, and with an eye for ever directed towards his own private interests. He possessed an inexhaustible flow of high-sounding words, and what he delighted to term 'a strident voice.' Indeed, when the said voice was 'turned on' there was no stopping it— no getting in a word edgewise—no hearing any other voice. He absolutely roared down everybody else, and, being very much of a bully, delighted to do so—this, too, with a shrewd purpose.

From the first moment of his entrance to the house he made it his aim to become its 'uncrowned king.' And, all things considered, he took the very best means of achieving his purpose.

To begin with, he was en rapport with the sympathies of the majority from the outset. His opinions on all matters, though generally much more advanced, were founded on the same data, and showed, if in sharper outline, the very same features as their own. They understood and approved of him; and, on his side, he thoroughly understood and approved of them. No man among them was likely to meet rebuke of his for sharp practice of any sort, but just the reverse, especially when the practitioner was saucy too. Consummate impudence, when he met with it, was exceedingly to his liking; and so, indeed, were most other qualities which honest people are accustomed to discountenance, provided always that their practice was duly artistic.

But Mr. Coppersmut, for all that, did not place himself among the people he wanted to join as an equal. Under all times and circumstances he insisted on posing before them as a thorough gentleman and an accomplished scholar; and here his gift of the gab' and his strident voice stood him in good stead. In connection with a trick of his—that of twisting every remark that fell from the lips of anybody who dared to broach independent opinions in his presence into an invidious meaning—they enabled him, in the view of the crowd, to claim superiority, intellectually speaking, over every one who came in contact with him.

Thus advising the mob as they liked to be advised, venting opinions certain to please them, and bullying those who disagreed into silence, Mr. Coppersmut soon attained his end, and was universally recognised as the uncrowned pauper-king of that particular workhouse.

In addition to his other qualities, Mr. Coppersmut was plausible and hypocritical more than any man I ever met, and just as vain. While flattering and wheedling the mob, he was just as eager to insinuate himself into the confidence of any one of higher standing whom he supposed might be rendered useful. He mostly succeeded, too, up to a certain point, until his inveterate turn for duping and making tools of everybody came into play, as it was sure to do at an early date, and thus rendered actively hostile persons who otherwise might have befriended him.

As to his vanity, he was always laying himself out for applause, and therefore always assuming precisely the attitude calculated to win it. His life, indeed, from the cradle had been one long scene of acting. His very gait and gestures, as well as such of his actions as came before the public, were all moulded to conciliate and gratify the lookers-on. He wanted to be taken for a good husband, a good father, a good citizen, a good Churchman, and a good friend—the best of all these, the one model man indeed. Thus he went about with a gracious smile for ever on his countenance, and with a sliding, insinuating tread, neither of which ever varied in the least, so long as eyes were upon him. Thus, too, his children were trained into greeting him before spectators as if he were the sole object of their admiration and affection. This kind of thing was carried out in the workhouse as duly as elsewhere. His children were taught to steal to him in the oakum-shed, or wherever he might be employed, and there embrace him with effusion for the edification of the rest of the male paupers; and most of them were edified accordingly into the deepest respect for the admirable Mr. Copper-smut.

As to his wife, now: such a man as Mr. Coppersmut—so able, so universally accomplished, such a perfect master of his profession, so gentlemanly, and so unexceptionable in all the relations of life—was bound to have a plausible excuse for sinking down from his former high estate into the condition of a pauper; and he could find no better excuse than—his wife. According to him, she was his very antipodes in all things, morally speaking, and the one sole cause of his ruin. Poor woman 1 it was quite true that she had her faults, and one a grave one: she drank. But it is easy to understand how a frank, straightforward, impetuous woman could be driven to drinking by such a man.

That he was chiefly to blame no sensible person who heard her husband descant on her vice and its consequence could doubt. There was no reluctance in him to disclose her shame; very much the contrary. He used to tell, with absolute exultation, how the youths of his neighbourhood—a very low one, by the way—and sheerly out of respect and sympathy for him, used to follow her about, hooting and hustling her, and likewise bedaubing her from head to foot with soot, flour, and red-ochre. While detailing this kind of thing, he never uttered a word in disapproval of the mob. It seemed to him the most natural thing in the world that they should do all this, and without the smallest interruption from anybody—least of all from him.

For my own part, however, when I reflected on the story, and on the manner of the teller, I was forced to conclude that he himself was the instigator of these blackguardly attacks on his own wife. This, too, before I became acquainted with his real character. These hootings, hustlings, and bedaubings of Mrs. Coppersmut served him well. They withdrew public attention from his own conduct and fastened it upon her. In consequence, they did much towards shifting the odium attending his ruin from himself to her.

And how, it will be asked, had his ruin really come about? In answering, I am bound to begin at the beginning. Mr. Coppersmut had held many appointments in his time, and invariably got on excellently in every one of them for two months or so. But then, having mastered the routine of the office and, if possible, a few secrets compromising to the firm, his worse qualities would assert themselves; he would attempt to oust the employés above him, to bully and browbeat his masters, and, if possible, to make dupes and tools of the clients, with the consequence that he was sure to be sent adrift, and that, too, in double-quick time. In short, he was always far too clever for himself; such an inveterate plotter and intriguer—and so unprincipled, too—that people never felt safe so long as he was connected with them.

So he had been going on for years, until at length he became so thoroughly known in the profession that no solicitor, reputable or the opposite, would have anything to do with him. Then he went into partnership with a fellow-clerk in much the same predicament as himself. These two, between them paying a solicitor out of practice for the use of his name, started a business of a peculiar kind.

It was not, however, by any means the only business of the same peculiar kind in existence, as the Incorporated Law Society,

I suspect, is aware. Its work, as I think, consisted chiefly in advising rogues how to evade the penalties of the law, and in finding shady clients for shady attorneys. And a good deal of the work, as in all similar cases, was done in taverns, between seven o'clock in the evening and closing time. The fact is suggestive.

The partnership, however, soon came to an end. The partner was the head of the firm, and Mr. Coppersmut lost no time in attempting to dupe, make a tool of, and reduce him to a secondary rank, with very secondary emolument, of course. It was his usual way. As usual, too, he was worsted in the encounter, and kicked—literally kicked out of the office; for among his other high qualities Mr. Coppersmut was very much of a cur.

Then he perpetrated a trick which swept away for ever such shreds of character as till then remained to him. His partner and himself had previously instituted an action against one of the shady firms to which they had introduced clients, in relation to commission; and Mr. Coppersmut had given evidence in the case in favour of self and partner, which secured them a verdict. Their opponents, however, moved for and obtained a new trial; and now that Mr. Coppersmut was no longer a member of the triumphant firm, he turned round and swore as strongly for the defendants as he had previously sworn against them.

It was an ill-advised act, done under the influence of vindictive passion, and utterly unlike Mr. Coppersmut's usual way. But even the cleverest of actors must be natural now and again in spite of themselves, and generally, as in this instance, to their own great loss and discomfiture.

The crash came immediately; but the man was prepared for it—after a fashion. He could not help foreseeing that the workhouse was destined to be his lot, for some time previously; and he was ready to make the best of it. Already one or two workhouse inmates of his own stamp had signalized themselves by bringing actions against boards of guardians in various parts of the country, and by gaining damages too; and Mr.

Coppersmut conceived that, could he but follow suit, he would be what is vulgarly called 'a made man.'

Indeed, so far as he could see, there was no other method of restoring himself to society open to him, since to obtain another situation was quite out of the question. Besides, damages were far more inviting than any situation could possibly be.

He had learned a thing or two while working with his late partner; and his one desire now was to establish a business of the same kind on his own account. It was such a delightful sort of business—conducted along such pleasant lines, in such pleasant times and places, and in the midst of such pleasant company—so fascinating, in short, that Mr. Coppersmut was quite willing to wait a year, or even two, foregoing all other offers and openings the while, if such waiting appeared at all likely to give the requisite capital for realizing his darling plan. To bring an action for damages against the guardians, and therefore to provoke them to some act or acts that would justify such an action, were precisely the ideas with which he made himself and family indoor paupers. And as a necessary preliminary, he had occupied his leisure, for months before, in learning all that could be learned, especially in the way of scandal, concerning the workhouse destined to be his refuge, its officers, and its board of guardians. Thus he became an inmate when pretty well primed; and, once inside, he found no difficulty in completing his information, especially as concerned the weak points in the system of management and in the characters of the managers.

I have already told how he won the mass of his fellow-paupers; and having obtained full control of them, it follows that their habitual peccadilloes were systemized, and extended also so far as they could be made to reach. The rogues among the inmates soon saw the benefit attending his uncrowned kingship, and became his followers heart and soul—a body ready to obey his behest wherever it was possible.

In a little time he succeeded in making, what he desired so earnestly, a case for an action for damages against the guardians.

131

In reward for his services, the firm of solicitors for which he had last sworn promised him temporary employment as a copyist, whenever they might need an extra hand in that capacity. They kept their word, too, once or twice before he entered the house and several times afterwards.

On the first of these several occasions, Mr. Coppersmut applied for leave to go out, in order to accept the job, his wife and family to be allowed the while to remain in the house until he could reconstruct his home—a thing which he assured the guardians he had a reasonable prospect of accomplishing, since he had been given to understand that the firm offering the job intended to take him permanently into their service, in case he gave satisfaction; and, he added, there could be no possibility of doubting his ability to do so.

Nor did the guardians doubt. Like most people in that quarter, they entertained the highest opinion of his native talents, business capacity, and integrity; and, like most people, they fully believed that his wife was the sole cause of his ruin. They pitied, it need scarcely be told, and were willing to aid him as far as lay in their power.

Our pettifogger obtained the permission requested, and went out to reconstruct his home.' The job lasted ten days, and was very well paid for. Coppersmut spent five or six days more, enjoying himself about town; then he returned to the house without a penny in his pocket, but with a well-constructed and exceedingly doleful tale in his mouth about disappointments and privations endured.

The guardians quite believed him; for they allowed him to go out twice more on precisely the same conditions as at first. During his third absence, however, certain things came to their knowledge, which made it perfectly clear how grossly the fellow had been imposing upon them. So, having first warned him to remove his wife and family within a certain time, they procured a warrant for his apprehension, on the charge of leaving them chargeable to the Union, brought him before a magistrate, and secured his committal to prison for some weeks—with hard labour.

On his release, he went straight back to the workhouse, and, a few days later, had the audacity to make a fourth application to the guardians of precisely the same sort as the other three. As before, he was going out to temporary employment; and as before, this temporary employment was sure to culminate in a permanent appointment.

The guardians refused, with something like indignation, to grant the brazen demand; and, hot on the refusal, Mr. Coppersmut sent them a very lawyer-like letter, pointing out the irreparable injury they had inflicted upon him, and demanding a large sum by way of compensation.

The last demand was treated with contempt; and, from that day forward, Mr. Coppersmut waged relentless war with workhouse officers and guardians.

His first care was to bring an action, in *formâ pauperis*, for damages, against the guardians. But, wide as was his acquaintance with legal forms and among sharp practitioners, he was months upon months before he could find a solicitor to take it up, and a barrister to give opinion as to its validity.

The time thus spent, however, was not lost—very far from it. He was now busy in tormenting the guardians in every way, and especially in provoking reprisals; and all these reprisals, no matter how justifiable on their part, were imported into his case as acts of gross tyranny and oppression. Nor was this all. If a guardian happened to make a remark concerning his case on board-day which the local papers thought fit to publish, a note was immediately made of it by Mr. Coppersmut, as defamation and slander for the consideration of his counsel.

With all this, he could not but feel that the case was rather a flimsy one at best, and therefore he employed every device known to him to bolster it. With this view, he set to work complaining of everything that could be complained of, except, of course, the malpractices of himself and his accomplices in the house. Thus, for months, there were Local Government inquiries every week or so into various abuses and defects connected with the establishment and in one or two cases Mr. Coppersmut scored very decided successes. These, it will be understood, could not fail to increase his influence in the house; and when at length he did find a lawyer to take up his case and open proceedings, he became far more powerful with his fellows than officers and guardians put together. This influence he used in various ways to promote his own ends. One of these ways was, to stimulate everybody who had the ghost of a grievance to place it before the Local Government Board in set form. Not that he cared a straw about the matter in dispute; but he reasoned, All these multiplied complaints, whether well founded or not, cannot fail to tell with a jury, and thus prejudice it in my favour. Further, the Local Government cannot help concluding, in the end, that there must be something very wrong in matters here, or we paupers would not be eternally complaining. Finally, officers and guardians will begin to fight shy of me, and thus pass over my incessant and flagrant breaches of discipline.'

The last conclusion of Mr. Coppersmut was perfectly accurate. Officers and guardians did fight very shy of him indeed, after his lawsuit was opened. They ceased to punish his ostentatious misconduct—or, indeed, to notice it at all. He was allowed to do very much as he pleased in the day-rooms and workshops; and it delighted him, above all things, to hold forth all day long in the loudest tones of his strident voice concerning the rights of paupers, the wrong-doings of guardians, and the proper legal methods of dealing with both. Nor did he fail, while thus engaged, to detail all the scandalous stories he had ever heard concerning guardians and officers, and to add a good many concocted by himself.

The more respectable inmates of the house soon got tired of this sort of thing; but there was no help for it. The pettifogger had things all his own way, and anybody who ventured to remonstrate was set down as an informer, and treated accordingly. Even when Coppersmut and his allies proceeded so far as to beat such a one by pre-arrangement, the whole thing was set aside by the master as a pauper brawl,' and the perpetrators of the assault, who, with their principal, richly deserved to be locked up, were allowed to go free. This gave .he finishing touch to Mr. Coppersmut's uncrowned kingship. His satellites looked upon him as invincible, and acted accordingly. And so did Mr. Coppersmut with respect to the satellites.

Law cannot be carried on without money, even in *formâ pauperis*,' was his constant cry; then turning to such of them as he knew to be possessed of a; few shillings he would add, lend me so-and-so, and I will pay you double when I get—my damages.'

They lent, too, as much as they could—every man of them — especially such as hoped that the pettifogger would assist them in bringing similar actions for damages against the guardians, so soon as his own had been satisfactorily disposed of; and there were no fewer than a dozen such in the house. 'Of course I will help you, and you shall win,' was his invariable remark to all of them; and it was believed with perfect faith.

Meanwhile Mr. Coppersmut, who was not quite so confident respecting the legal issue of the affair, was doing his best to make it profitable in another way. Once a week he quitted the house regularly, dragging wife and children at his heels. At the gate he sent them one way to beg, with a cleverly drawn-up petition and subscription-list in their hands, while he went in another, seeking somebody with more money than brains who could be induced to advance him a handsome loan on his prospective damages. The latter were set down at several hundreds, which was one argument in his favour; the opinion of his counsel was another; and, finally, there was his own most artful and unscrupulous statement.

Many were the rebuffs he met with; but Mr. Coppersmut never lost heart. Morally speaking, his hide was thicker than that of the lamented Jumbo. It was impervious to everything in the shape of repulse or insult. At length, just a fortnight or so before the day fixed for the trial, he did meet with a credulous simpleton of means—one, it is fair to say, no less greedy than credulous, as will soon appear; and to this man Mr. Coppersmut mortgaged the whole of his damages for half the amount at which they had been rated. This much success achieved, the pettifogger very quietly levanted, leaving his wife and children to the care of the guardians, by way of remembrancers.

Chapter XIII.
Conclusion.

A PROVERB, very well known and frequently in the mouth of the classes to which it refers, tells us that 'Poverty is no crime.' I assert that in a great many instances this is erroneous—that poverty is a crime quite serious enough to be visited by legal penalties of considerable severity.

I say nothing here of casuals or vagabonds; I confine myself exclusively to indoor paupers. And of these most assuredly the habitual Ins and Outs ought to be dealt with as criminals. Such a course will have to be adopted with them sooner or later; and the sooner the better. For the sake of everybody, including themselves, they must not be allowed to remain as they are.

I further assert that the very act of making their practice a criminal offence would at once reclaim a great number of them; and that the additional act of carrying out firmly a sufficient enactment levelled at them would practically rid society of them. I have the best authority for this statement—*their own*. I have put it to them again and again, and still again—numberless times, in fact; and in every instance the answer has been to this effect If there were judicious and well-administered laws affecting us, we would soon cease to exist.' The truth is, In-and-Outism is but an acute form of Casualism; and it is acute simply because it is far more pleasant to play at the former than at the latter.

Next to the evil of the Ins and Outs is that attending the presence of lads of sixteen and upwards in the workhouse. If I possessed the power, this evil would not exist for an hour. I would remove them at any cost.

As to the mature, it has often struck me as remarkable that among our multitudinous benevolent associations there is not a single one for aiding deserving indoor paupers before it be too late. Every workhouse contains such; but, in my opinion, a pauper becomes hopeless as a subject of benevolence who has

137

spent any time in the place, or who has been in the habit of entering it occasionally.

However, married men with families, who enter after a hard struggle with adversity, are deserving objects, and ought to be assisted out. It is almost impossible for them to recover independence unaided. If a man tries to do so, he must go out, dragging his family at his heels. He has no home where he can leave them while he goes in search of employment. Such a search can hardly be successful in any case immediately, and least of all in this; and the man with a family at his heels, all in the streets and without resources of any kind, is just the man of all others who cannot protract his expedition; he is bound to return to the house with his family in a very few hours. The motto of such a man is, 'Once a pauper, always a pauper.' This should not be: it is a disgrace to any social system.

I have studiously avoided enlarging on the grievances continually in the mouths of paupers, because I find them nearly always groundless. Still paupers have their grievances, and very serious one; but, curiously enough, it is these that, as a rule, they wholly ignore. One never hears them complaining of what really furnishes subject of complaint. Among them, at least, it is a law of nature that *what weighs equally on everybody ceases to be a grievance to individuals.*

There is, however, another reason for their strange forbearance respecting the very trying grievance involved in depredations in their food. That such depredations are common, at least in this particular house, I can testify. I am notoriously the smallest eater among its males. The dole, though altogether insufficient for most, is more than enough for me: when I receive it undiminished, I never finish the whole. Yet I, more times than I can count, have felt what it was to have an unsatisfied stomach. What must it have been with others? Yesterday (Thursday), for instance, the pea-soup was measured short to every man in my set. The soup, too, was about as poor as soup could be; and yet immediately after dinner the pantrymen were selling basins, full to the brim, and anything rather than thin, to those who could afford to buy. It was shameful. But, I regret to say, such things are the rule.

Another abuse which indoor paupers never think worth notice is this:—There are men here who are doing absolutely nothing save nursing comfortable little fortunes. There are others, also, whose sole business is to qualify for pensions from charities to which their birth, in conjunction with pauperism, entitles them, but who, were it otherwise, could maintain themselves in very good style outside. Yet these men are precisely those who meet with the best treatment. The questions, as to their conduct, and by whom connived at, are well worth sifting.

But the most poignant abuse of the workhouse—that is, to sensitive minds—is the way in which its pauper inmates are regarded by the officers. They are not esteemed as human beings at all by these high and mighty gentry, but as creatures of a far inferior order—of less account, indeed, than the tenants of a kennel. They are spoken to and treated as if they had no feelings whatever, but were merely so much rubbish encumbering the establishment and giving its staff a world of unnecessary trouble.

For these and all other workhouse evils I see but one remedy. That, however, seems to me a very sufficient one. It is a mistake and something more—in many cases a crime—to draw boards of guardians from a single class, and that one the class of tradesmen. These people cannot be induced to regard anything save class and personal interests. To keep down the rates, especially in their own cases—to bring the average sum per head for the maintainance of indoor paupers to the lowest possible point—to favour friends in the bestowal of contracts—to place convenient vassals in comfortable posts, and to favour dubious people in the house and out—these are their leading principles, with in many cases a few others, almost unnecessary to name, but of which certain investigations which took place into certain irregularities occurring in workhouses during the past year will give my readers an idea.

The best remedy for all these abuses, I venture to suggest, would be found in boards of guardians containing a fair proportion of working men. Men who have relatives and former comrades in the house would unquestionably keep a sharp eye on abuses likely to pain their friends, and a still sharper eye upon them if they felt that they were themselves ever likely to 'come to the Union.' That is obvious. Guardians of this stamp would extinguish at once the insolence of Jacks in office, and the corruption and depredation which no system of management and no strictness of discipline can deal with effectually as things stand. It would secure poor pauper inmates treatment a little more worthy of a Christian land. Nor would this be its only good. Working men guardians would detect, far quicker than others, impostors who seek to prey upon the rates. They would be just the men, also, to deal with the skulking Ins and Outs as they merited. Where they had a voice in such matters, there would be no placing of cast mistresses, complaisant husbands, or needy relatives in pleasant posts. Above all they would keep a tight hand, though not a whit tighter than was absolutely necessary, over relieving officers—a class of parochial officials notorious in town and country for giving way to the temptations peculiarly incident to their position.

It may be urged that recent changes in our political system will of itself give us such guardians. I say, No; nothing will do it save legislation, stipulating in plain terms that such and such a proportion of the members of every board of guardians must be working men—householders, if it be preferred, but still working men residing in the Union.

It need not be dreaded that such men will be too extravagant. On the contrary, there are many reasons for supposing that they will positively reduce the expenditure; and several of these reasons I have glanced at.

One word more. A great number of employers are at the present moment, as for some time past, busily engaged in increasing the number of indoor paupers. These persons consider that a workman is completely used up by the time he attains his forty-fifth year. They give, therefore, directions to their foremen that no man past that age shall be engaged in their factories.

The order is a cruel one; but it seems to me no less injudicious than cruel. Age does not reckon merely by years; there is many a man of sixty far stronger and more efficient in every respect than men of forty or under. Experience, too, should count for something. The man of widest experience, it will generally be admitted, other things being equal, must surpass a younger rival in value to a master.

I have a striking instance within reach of me at this very moment. The man is a millwright, over sixty, but gifted with a powerful frame and a fine constitution. He is still hale and hearty, and as capable of a trying day's work as most men. He has brains, too, and some education; and he has served in the foremost engineering establishments of the United States, as well as in those of England. He has even had spells in various foreign dockyards. T here is no new method or improvement in any department of his profession with which he is not familiar. He has ways of his own, also, in effecting different kinds of work which materially decrease the toil and difficulty incident to them. Having always taken a deep interest in machinery, I may be presumed competent to give an opinion here. This man returned from the States some years ago, to attend the death-bed of his last surviving child, with plenty of money in his pocket. Having buried the child, he had no heart to leave the country any more, so set about procuring employment. Everybody was aware that no better workman existed; but the general answer to his application ran, 'You were born too soon'—a piece of workshop irony meaning that the applicant belonged to the past generation rather than the present, and was ineligible for employment.

Meanwhile his money melted away. And here he is—absolutely eating his strong heart out with vexation, because, though still full of strength of body and brain, he is condemned to a life of uselessness and stagnation. His is a typical case. There are scores, absolutely scores, of fine workmen round me, with plenty of life in them yet, condemned to indoor pauperism merely because, in workshop slang, they were 'born too soon.'

Silly as well as selfish employers! How many times over is not the labour of hours, and even of whole days, on the part of hundreds of men lost to them, simply because there is no man of experience at hand to show how a number of unusual operations ought to be performed.

This selfish—I might well call it insane—trick of masters, in driving men over forty-five into the workhouse, cannot be too widely known and reprobated. It is, however, a trick that has actually been adopted by the Government. It is the rule in all Government dockyards and factories, that no man over forty-five shall be taken on.

Thus our modern *Christian* and *Economical* way of reasoning is that—when a handy craftsman wants work, he is too old for it after forty-five; and that when he wants rest, he is too young for it until he passes sixty. Thus, during the intervening fifteen years or more, according to the pleasure of Poor Law Guardians and Employers, he is forbidden either to work or rest.

THE END.

Printed in Great Britain
by Amazon.co.uk, Ltd.,
Marston Gate.